# Worldly Wanderlust: Unforgettable Travel Guides

Weronika .W French

## *Funny helpful tips:*

*In the symphony of life, play your part with passion and authenticity.*

*Invest in research and insights; they drive informed business decisions.*

*Worldly Wanderlust: Unforgettable Travel Guides : Roam the Globe: Unforgettable Globetrotting Tips and Adventure-Fueled Travel Guides*

## _Life advices:_

_Stay agile in business strategies; adaptability ensures resilience._

_Stay reflective; learning from the past provides insights for the future._

# Introduction

This is a comprehensive manual that aims to equip individuals with the necessary knowledge and strategies to embark on a journey around the world confidently. It begins by addressing common fears associated with travel, providing practical advice on how to overcome them, and promoting a positive mindset conducive to an enjoyable and fulfilling travel experience.

The guide also offers valuable insights into traveling on a budget, including tips on saving money, working overseas, and managing finances efficiently while exploring different destinations. It emphasizes the benefits of solo travel, providing guidance on how to make the most of the experience and meet new people along the way.

Moreover, the guide provides an in-depth exploration of various types of travel destinations, including beaches, jungles, mountains, ancient ruins, and bustling cities, offering readers valuable information on the unique experiences these places can offer.

Furthermore, the guide offers practical advice on booking flights, narrowing down destinations, and utilizing websites to save money. It also provides comprehensive information on lodging options, transportation methods, and safety measures to ensure a secure and enjoyable travel experience. Additionally, the guide addresses essential aspects such as packing, preparing for the plane journey, and managing various travel-related documents and requirements.

The guide also offers valuable insights into cultural awareness and respect, providing advice on how to interact with locals and immerse oneself in different cultures while respecting local customs and traditions. Lastly, it includes tips for meeting people, engaging with locals, and getting the most out of a travel experience, ensuring that readers are well-prepared for a transformative and enriching journey around the world.

# Contents

# Chapter 1

## Overcoming Fear

*"When we step out, with trusting hearts, into the unknown, we become magnets for blessings!"*

- Jessica Donley, New Orleans, USA

Them: "Will you sing for us? On stage? Tomorrow night?"
Us: "But we can't sing!"
Them: "We don't care."
Us at the same time: "Yes!" "No!"

My friend and I decided to live and travel around China for six months, and nothing could have prepared us for the crazy experiences we had. We taught English and were placed in a small town outside a small city where many people had never seen a foreigner before.

The second we stepped out of our apartment door, we were treated like mini-celebrities. People stared, pointed, took pictures and videos of us, and they frequently asked for pictures with us. They would pull over if they were driving, hand us their kids, take pictures of us even if we were eating, follow us and comment on everything we did. Although there were times when the attention was overwhelming, for the most part, we didn't mind because it gave us so many great stories.

At one point during our stay, we decided to try a new restaurant. We were prepared for the attention we knew we'd get, but nothing could have prepared us for the request that followed.

After saying yes, my friend looked at me like, "WHAT?!" I told her, "We have to; it's just too good to pass up."

So the next day, we found ourselves on stage belting out Lady Gaga, Justin Bieber and Celine Dion in front of an entire restaurant. They gave us free food, free beer, and they kept us entertained the whole time. We were relieved to find out they didn't actually want us on stage the entire time, they just wanted us to put on a show. We were asked to dance, smile, speak Mandarin and even walk around, while singing and waving at everyone. A ton of people took pictures with us, children made us gifts out of napkins and families put food at our feet. It was nuts! We have some videos of the night and even though our voices sounded terrible, the audience seemed to love us anyway.

We could have stayed home and remained "Safe." We could have remained in our comfort zone and allowed our fear of what others would think to stop us. But we didn't.

Now, when we look back, neither of us can imagine not having that as part of our experience in China. The feeling of "Did we just do that?!" was worth every bit of nerves and anxiety that we felt beforehand.

"You must be so brave."

Me?! When people tell me this, I find myself laughing. They clearly don't know me. I am afraid of so many things! I have thrown numerous ice cream cones in the air because a bee wanted some too. I once ran out of a hotel in Bali in my underwear and pounded on my neighbor's window because a massive spider was doing circus tricks in my room. EVERY time I get on a plane I feel apprehensive.

I now recognize apprehension as a disguise for fear. Fear is a sneaky emotion and masks itself with all sorts of other emotions and makes excuses such as, "When I get older;" "It's on my bucket list;" or "I haven't had time to book it." These may be legitimate reasons, but not if they're used to procrastinate on a dream.

Fear runs through us all, whether we are aware of it or not. If we are aware of it, we can use it to our advantage and press forward. If we are not mindful of it, it will make decisions on our behalf and keep us from reaching our full potential. Traveling can be scary, especially if you are going alone or to somewhere new. If you don't want fear to rule your life, you need to learn to recognize it when it manifests.

What fears do you have that might keep you from traveling?

## How to Overcome Your Fears

**Fear of Flying:** I'm going to let you in on a secret. We are all afraid of flying. Oh, sure, we look calm when the plane takes off. Some of us read books, some of us fall asleep because gravity makes us drowsy (or is that just me?), but deep inside, we all pray that we are not one of the few who find themselves in the improbable event of a water landing.

It is the same reason we feel uneasy in the car when someone else is driving. We are out of control. Our safety is no longer in our hands; it is in the hands of technology and a pilot who is hopefully not also drowsy upon take-off. I am sure you know that you are much safer in the air than on the ground, but it's still an uneasy feeling. I have a few recommendations that may help, depending on how severe your fear is:

- Take a flight preparation class. There are classes around the country that help prepare those who have a fear of flying.

- Drink some alcohol before you get on the plane. Sometimes, a drink calms the nerves and takes the edge off. Just make sure not to drink too much. You do not want to be that person. I once saw a drunk lady scream her head off because a flight attendant took her bag to put it up into the storage bin. She was slurring, trying to stand up, and kept going on and on about the flight attendant stealing her stuff. Yikes!

- Take a sleeping pill. If your flight is long enough, you may want to consider using supplements, medicine, or teas to help you sleep.

- Listen to calming or meditative music. Put your earbuds in and take deep breaths until you feel calmer.

- Chat with your seat neighbor. Typically, I prefer not to talk, but there are a few people I have met on planes that I am still friends with to this day. I'm still waiting to meet Mr. Right this way. ;)

- Inform the staff if you feel scared. I have a friend who tells the attending staff that he has a hard time flying, and they are generally more than willing to help him, in whatever way possible.

## Fear of Feeling Unsafe

As a solo female traveler, safety is always on my mind. I research the places I am going, the safest ways to travel within those countries, and the dangers I may face while there. The research helps alleviate my fear. I tend to follow some basic rules, which I will go into in the safety chapter.

When you are experiencing something out of your comfort zone, it will always seem scary at first. *Feeling* safe is often mistaken for *being* safe, but this is not always true as they are not the same thing. I have several well-meaning friends and family members who worry for me when I am gone, even though I am statistically safer than when I am at home.

Think of it this way. There is a vast source of knowledge out there. If you choose to stay in your comfort zone, you will never be able to tap into it. There is no way to do it from the place you are from; no amount of Google, YouTube, or pictures can help you gain it. You need to experience the knowledge to attain it. Every time you decide to be brave and leave your comfort zone, you learn SO MUCH. This can be as small as trying something new where you live or as big as traveling to a new place.

Fear can seriously limit your education and potential for growth. What it cannot do, however, is guarantee safety in your comfort zone, outside of it, or straddling the line. You may as well do the things you long to do, plan to be as safe as possible while doing them and move forward into an exciting and full life.

If you are a first-time traveler and the thought of traveling to a new place scares you, I would recommend going somewhere familiar. Choose a location that speaks your language or a famous place like Paris, London, or Rome. If safety is a big concern, here is a list of the safest cities in the world according to the Safe City Index.

The world's safest cities for 2021
1. Tokyo, Japan
2. Singapore
3. Osaka, Japan
4. Amsterdam, the Netherlands
5. Sydney, Australia
6. Toronto, Canada
7. Washington DC, US
8. Copenhagen, Denmark
9. Seoul, South Korea
10. Melbourne, Australia

## Fear of Feeling Stupid or Inadequate

I would love to write some corny and inspiring message telling you that you won't feel this way, but honestly, there is no getting around this one. You may as well embrace it because if you are in a new place, you will feel stupid, at least once. It is part of the humor of traveling.

Once, I was desperately trying to leave a grocery store in Norway, but there were gates in the way. I tried multiple things to get out, but to no avail. Finally, a clerk came up to me with an annoying smirk on his face and showed me how to get out. He spoke to me like I was a child as he showed me how to put my receipt up to a scanner to leave. I could not help but laugh, despite his tone, and tell him, "I would never have gotten out of here!"

## Fear of People Who Aren't Like You

Whether we are aware of it or not, we are not comfortable with people who are not like us. It doesn't matter what color our skin is, our religion, country or sub-culture; if we are in a group of people different from us, we are all likely to feel uncomfortable.

The first step to overcoming this kind of fear is to be aware of it and how it affects the choices we make. If you hesitate to travel to certain countries because the culture is so different from yours, I encourage you to explore your reasons. The more you seek to understand yourself, the more likely you are to overcome it and eventually travel to these places.

It's also important to note that there is nothing wrong with being uncomfortable. It's a common and normal feeling. It can even be motivating, if we approach it with a sense of curiosity instead of using it as a reason to avoid or judge others. We should ask questions, put our own beliefs aside, and listen. The more we learn, the more that discomfort eases. Try to see that feeling as a good thing!

## Fear of Language Barriers

Gestures go a long way. I've been all over the world, gesturing, pointing, smiling, waving, and bowing. I also try to learn the following words before I travel; *Hello, Thank you, Please, Sorry, Where, and Beer*. Honestly, what more do you need?

If you speak English, you have a significant advantage in the traveling world. English is the universal language and will be used in most airports and major hotels. However, please do not readily assume everyone will speak to you in English. Use Google translate or have a language guide ready. I always start with translation because I do not want to be arrogant, assuming everyone speaks English; however, people often switch to English once they realize I don't speak the language.

The key is to just try. Like my friend Anna from New Zealand says, *"Don't be afraid to go somewhere you don't know the language. You can start with a thumbs up, pointing, and a smile."*

## Fear of the First Step

The hardest part of any trip? Booking the tickets. The decisions and apprehension of the unknown can feel overwhelming. Every step after that feels a little bit better. Although, I've booked many trips, I'm an anxious person and I always have a sense of unease when I'm booking a ticket. I try to be aware of it, accept it as part of the process, and keep moving forward.

Just book the ticket!

# Chapter 2

## Bucket List Mentality

*"Stop dreaming about your bucket list and start living it!"*

-Annette White

While in China, my friend and I visited a gorgeous town called Guilin and met a vivacious girl from Chile named Belen. Belen is engaging and her zest for life and sense of humor are contagious. We toured the area together for a few days and found ourselves in hilarious situations. One of the funniest experiences came from a night of clubbing. Everyone was sitting in booths around a stage, but no one was dancing. Belen decided she wanted to dance and dragged another guy and me up on stage, and the next thing I knew, I was showing off my terrible dance moves in front of an entire club. At one point, a bunch of people got up on stage with us, and somehow, I ended up in the center of a dance circle. My friend, outside of the circle, was dying laughing and kept taking pictures of me dancing awkwardly for my "fans."

One of the most memorable things about Belen is that she was a lawyer at home. She had a serious job and saved for an entire year to travel the world. She told me that her employers tried to convince her that the trip was a bad idea and that she may not have a job when she returned, but she knew she needed to take the trip. Instead of listening to others' doubts, she worked her butt off, and when the time came, she traveled all over the world with no regrets. After her trip, she returned home and was able to get her old job back. Her story stands out to me because she is someone who followed through on her desire to travel. She's an inspiration because she didn't just SAY she wanted to do it - she carefully put in the work to make her dream happen.

Bucket List Mentality is when someone wishes he or she could do something, but instead of actually doing it, it sits on a list to be referenced but never fulfilled. Bucket lists can be extremely useful *if you are actively working at completing the items on your list.* It gets people thinking about things they hope to accomplish, and if used correctly, holds them accountable.

However, sometimes, there is a particular pattern with people who say "It's on my Bucket List."

1. Someone says, "I want to do that." And puts it on a bucket list.

2. The person feels rewarded for being the kind of person who would want to do said thing.

3. The person never does it.

People with Bucket List Mentality use bucket lists as wish lists instead of to-do lists. For many, having Bucket List Mentality is fine because they just like to dream, and they won't be upset if they don't get most of it accomplished. For others, this list has at least one or two things they deeply desire but don't address because they hope to get to it someday. In this case, it can become more of a regret list, a failure list, or even a stress list.

If you DO decide to keep a bucket-list here are some suggestions to make the list more attainable:

**1. Focus on just one or two goals**

You can make your list as long or as short as you want but choose one or two items on your list to work on until you get them accomplished. Doing this allows you to prioritize the ones most important to you, and it can make the list seem less overwhelming.

## 2. Write your list down and keep it somewhere visible

You can make this a simple list on a piece of paper taped on your fridge or as complex as a vision board with mind-maps and timelines of how you will accomplish each one.

## 3. Break down your goals into small steps

After you've chosen one or two items to focus on, break them down into steps. If your goal is to go to Ireland, these are some of the first steps you might choose to take.

1. Research flights

2. Ask for Time Off

3. Book Flight Tickets

4. Research Lodging Options

5. Book Lodging

Again, I suggest writing these steps down, making them visible, and crossing them off as you finish each task. Not only will it help you complete it, but it also feels fantastic to cross things off of a to-do list.

## 4. Give yourself a deadline for each item

Think of a realistic date for completing items. Once you've broken the steps down, you can give each one a deadline as well. Deadlines help create a sense of urgency that can override the need to procrastinate. Even if you do not meet all your deadlines, think of it as motivation that helps get you there sooner.

1. Research flights (by Monday)

2. Ask for Time Off (by next Friday)

3. Book Tickets (by two weeks from today)

## 5. Get an accountability partner

1. Ask a friend or family member to hold you accountable. There are a few ways that others can help you stay on track. Plan to meet up with an accountability partner to discuss progress

2. Have someone text you regularly to see how it is going

3. Post the step's deadlines on social media

4. Create calendar event reminders or alarms on your phone

5. Sign up on an accountability website

## 6. Make an annual bucket list rather than a life-time bucket list

I have a friend that does this every year on her birthday, and she does all sorts of cool things throughout the year, trying to meet the deadline for the next birthday.

## What are some ways you can hold yourself accountable for your travel dreams?

If you are someone who doesn't necessarily have a bucket-list, but you like the idea of keeping track of the things you want to do, you may find use in things like vision boards, habit trackers, life-coaches, meetup groups, or planners. Try to decide exactly what has held you back from accomplishing what you want to get done and steps you can take to overcome it.

Even with all the preparation, no amount of planning can undo the fact that you simply may not be able to do what you set out to do. Either be prepared to try again in the future, or just be thankful for what you learned along the way.

# Chapter 3

## How to Travel on a Budget

*"You don't have to be rich to travel; some of the best experiences can be found with people you meet in a hostel dorm or campground."*

- Anna, New Zealand

A few years ago, after a particularly challenging year, I spontaneously decided to go to Europe and travel for a while. I moved out of my apartment and estimated what it would cost to travel, and then compared it to what I'd typically be spending on rent and living at home. My budget was about $1,400.00 month, or $45.00/day. I immediately paid for my two major flights and found one-way tickets for $250.00 each. At first on my trip, I spent too much money, but I soon found a rhythm and was able to average it all out to the daily budget.

One of the biggest things about traveling like this is being extra grateful for things such as a free meal or a free place to stay.

The first time I met Anne, I was walking to a mall in Tokyo. She came up to me and asked, "Are you American?" I looked down at my sweatshirt and jeans and jokingly asked, "What gave it away?" We quickly became friends. She is an incredible woman - half-Japanese and half-Dane and lives a really cool life. During my stay in Tokyo, we hung out a few times.

Fast forward a few years, to when I was going to be passing through Denmark. I reached out to her to see if she would want to meet up. She said yes and offered me a free place to stay in her little town. Not only did she let me stay a couple of nights, she let me do laundry and cooked for me while I was there. Anne also connected me with a friend of hers who was driving to Germany, who gave me a free ride to Hamburg. There was no way for me to repay the kindness other than saying, "Thank you!" a million times. They both assured me that they had been in my shoes, so they were simply paying it forward.

And now when a traveler comes through my city, I show the same consideration that was once shown to me.

I get asked ALL THE TIME how I afford to travel. People either think I make a ton of money or that I'm in a ton of debt. Neither is true. These days, I'm in a better financial position, and $45.00 a day is unnecessary; however, I still don't need much more than that and I tend to stick to the same amount. You don't need a lot of money to be a traveler; you just have to have the desire and the courage to go.

If I can travel overseas and live on a $1400.00 a month budget, you can certainly go on a $1,400.00 budget for a week or two. Save $100.00 a month, and you can go in 14 months. Save $200.00 a month and you can go in 7 months.

Here are key ways to save money:

- Plan your trips around flight deals

- Sleep in affordable lodging

- Limit tourist activities to the ones that you REALLY want to do

- Eat street food, cheap restaurants, or make your own food.

- Travel using a carry-on.

## Your Mindset

Everywhere you go, and everywhere you look, you are being sold the message that you "deserve" more. "Treat yourself;" "You've worked hard;" "Self-Care…" You get the idea. And while I agree that taking care of yourself is important, I think we should be aware that oftentimes, we are only being manipulated into buying something. Sometimes, going with the basic option IS self-care and sometimes that basic option IS treating yourself. It allows you to save money, to afford the trip, and to take more trips in the future.

Keep this in mind when you are searching for travel deals. They will always try to sell you the idea that you deserve more than the basic hotel or restaurant option you just chose.

I've never returned home from a trip and said, "Gee, I sure wish I would have spent more money on hotels, expensive restaurants, and alcohol."

Budgeting may be the only way you ever get to experience the world around you. Keep an open mind, and don't let anyone tell you that you are deprived because you are not spending more money. There are times I choose to splurge on things such as sitting down in a restaurant to enjoy a pretty view. However, I have found that I often enjoy looking at the same lovely view with a simple sandwich and beer from a local store, just as much.

## Traveling doesn't have to be overindulgent.

People from my home, the United States, tend to view traveling as a luxury experience. It is why so many assume that I must be making and spending a ton of money to be somewhere else. But most of the world does not view traveling this way. They view it as an educational experience. They are there to learn, grow, and have new experiences. Spending money and overindulging are not goals; therefore, they can afford to take many more trips. When I've met other U.S. citizens while traveling, a common subject that comes up is the process of learning how to experience the world without unnecessary spending.

## The Off-Beaten Path

*"Living a champagne life on a lemonade budget."* This is one of my favorite quotes. It perfectly describes how one can have full, rich, extraordinary and life-changing experiences on a budget.

When you travel, try to research creative ways to experience the place you are visiting. For example, I wanted to visit Florence, Italy. I was looking up hostels, and I noticed a highly rated hostel on *hostelworld.com* boasting to be in the heart of Tuscany. After reading the reviews and researching, I decided to go there instead of staying in the city. I arrived and found a beautiful hostel in the small town of Certaldo.

The hostel offered bike rides, wine tours and cooking classes. It even had a pool. When I got there, I was delighted to find a beautiful hostel that was once a monastery. It dated back to the end of the 14th century. I quickly met other travelers, and we spent the next couple of days hanging out together. I would never have been able to experience this if I had limited myself to Florence.

To many, it seems that traveling on a budget is limiting, but it tends to open up doors and possibilities that a traveler would never have thought of if they had a lot of money to spend at more popular places. Some of my more authentic traveling experiences have come from trying to budget and needing a different option.

## Long-Term Traveling

When I was at a Spanish school in San Carlos, Colombia, I met a wonderful woman named Emily. Emily was 39 at the time and had just started her travels in South America. She quickly became one of the favorites in my travel journeys, not only because she was close to my age but because she was relatable and honest.

Two remarkable things about her stood out to me. First, she was scared of bugs and wasn't too sure about "nature," but the first place she decided to travel on her journey was to the Colombian jungles. Talk about brave. I don't love bugs either, and at one point, we were both screaming and climbing all over everyone in a tight space, trying to get away from a huge cockroach that was crawling behind our heads. We laughed and swore and someone had to remove it for us before we could sit down and act like normal human beings.

The next amazing thing about her is that she quit her long-term job to travel. She saved up enough money to travel for at least five months then quit. It's the story that everyone wishes they had enough guts to carry out. I'm using her story to motivate any reader who desperately wants to do something like this. When Emily was finished traveling, she returned home and got a new job. You can too!

Long-term traveling is much cheaper than the average person realizes, depending on where you go and where you choose to sleep. If you decide to go this route, don't forget to factor in how much you normally spend on day-to day things like food, rent, going out, and utilities.

1. Check your car insurance for storage options

2. Put your stuff in storage and move out of your place

3. Rent your house out to someone

4. Go through all your monthly bills and decide if you can eliminate any while you are gone, such as the gym, subscriptions, delivery services, and more.

If you are going to Europe, $45/day is a pretty tight budget. It was worth it for me, but if living frugally does not sound appealing to you, you will find that money goes a lot further in places such as South America and Southeast Asia.

## Determining a Budget

Trying to determine what budget is right for you can be confusing, especially when you are listening to an experienced traveler tell you that she travels on what might seem like an impossibly small amount. If you are someone who is new to all of this there are a few things I want to point out.

1. Deciding what budget is best for YOU takes practice and time.

2. Your budget will vary depending on how you like to travel and where you are going.

I hesitate to give figures, because your traveling desires and experiences will be different from my own. I can tell you that you can easily travel in cheap countries for $800-1500 a month, but these numbers will depend heavily on things like:

- **How much you spend on plane tickets.**

- Use Chapter 6 to help you choose cheaper tickets

- **What kind of lodging you choose and how long you'll stay.**

- Read chapter 7 for lodging ideas

- **How much money you spend on food and drinks.**

- Research the average cost of meal or drink in the country you are wanting to visit.

- **What kind of activities and tours you do.**

- Research travel blogs to see how other travelers kept their costs down in the same place.

This is an example of how someone **could** choose to spend money on a trip. These numbers are ROUGH estimates of a trip to

Hanoi, Vietnam. The prices will vary depending on which country you go to, but it gives you an idea of how much cheaper traveling could be if you want to try.

I'd recommend researching on the internet, "Travel budget for _____(name of country)" or "Cheap travel in___."

**priceoftravel.com** is a great resource for this.

| | Cheap | Middle | Expensive |
|---|---|---|---|
| **Plane tickets** | PHX-LA $115 LA-Hanoi $450 Booked separately to save money. | PHX- Hanoi $850 (More expensive when booked on one search) | PHX-Hanoi $1,250+ Fastest and nicest airline offered |
| **Lodging** | Hostels $5-15/ night | Basic Hotel $40-70/night | Nice hotel 100+/ night |
| **Food** | Street Food, Grocery Stores, and the Occasional cheap restaurant $3-7/ a meal | Restaurants, some nicer than others $5-10 per meal | All Restaurants 10+/meal |
| **Activities** | Walk, Free-walking Tours, a tourist activity $0-$10.00 a day | Scheduled Tours One or two big expense activities (such as zip-lining, Ha Long Bay cruise etc.) $25-100 a day | Mostly bigger activities $50+/day |
| **Transportation** | Buses, metros, Tuk Tuk, walking, $0-10 a day | Taxis, tour buses $5-20 a day | Private Cars $40+ |

# How to Save?

- Consider getting a side job such as serving, tutoring, nannying, warehouse jobs, seasonal jobs. If working many hours seems overwhelming, remember it's just short term and will be well worth it when you are strolling around in a foreign land.

- Keep track of your spending. We spend far more than we realize on a daily basis. Cutting back on a few expenses, such as the gym, coffee, or going out to eat, can really make an impact on your savings.

- Download a spending app and stick to it. I use a simple app called *"Daily Budget."* I use it to keep track of my spending outside of monthly bills. There are detailed budget apps out there, but I won't use them if they take too much time.

- Ask your employer to take some money out of your check and put it directly into a separate savings account. I keep a "Travel Fund" account at a completely different bank. My paycheck is automatically divided, and I don't even look at the savings account until I'm ready to travel.

## Working Overseas

One of the most popular ways to work overseas is to teach English. In some countries, you will need a bachelor's degree for higher-paying jobs, but just being a native English speaker works in others - and some don't even require that. Eslcafe.com is a great way to research these kinds of jobs.

If you are hoping to get hired somewhere you can find positions at websites like www.workingtraveler.com Kareeve.com If you are unable to find a position this way, the best way to get hired is to go to the country and try to find work in any way you can. You are looking for local references to get your foot in the door. Hostels are some of the best sources of information and a great place to start.

## Working Remotely

Working remotely is more of an option than most realize. For some, it means convincing an employer that you can get the job done in another place for a few weeks or so. For many though, it means getting the courage to venture on your own with your particular skill set. Writing, marketing services, data analysis, web development, editing, health/life coaching, vlogging, and so much more. If you've worked in a certain industry for many years, chances are that you have some kind of skill that others need. You just need to learn how to get it online. Try researching this by typing in, "How to work remotely by_."

## Try This…

I once completed an activity that has stuck with me and is part of the reason I'm writing this book. Write a list of 50-100 things that you like doing. After you are done, go back and write down a way that you could make money doing each thing. After you've completed this you choose the few that stand out to you and start researching ways to make the dream come true.

## Work-away

If you are looking for an extended trip but not sure how you can afford it, workaways are among the most popular methods of maintaining the backpacking travel lifestyle. These kinds of experiences typically offer a place to sleep, and some even provide food. Work-away experiences include, hostel work, language schools, working with animals, working on farms, working in gardens, construction, campsites, festivals, eco-homes, etc. There are TONS of different volunteering experiences to choose.

This is how people travel for dirt cheap for long periods of time. It's the secret to how your friend Joe was able to disappear in Europe for five years. Many people start with one and get so addicted that they don't stop traveling for years. I've never done one, but I've met many travelers who have and are thankful for the experience.

While researching, make sure you don't "pay to go." For example, all over the internet, you'll see things like **"Volunteer as an English teacher and live like a local with a family!"** *Only $2,200.* I promise there are cheaper ways to see a place and experience the culture. These are not work-away programs; they are placement programs designed to make money. Totally different.

For more information on work-away programs, please see the Extra section. It is the last piece of advice, by a fascinating traveler named Elinor from the UK and Denmark. Here is a little bit of what she has to say.

"For me at least, the biggest benefit has been the people I've met through it. And since you've got food and accommodation covered, Work-away programs allow you to stay somewhere for 2 weeks, a month (or even 6 months in my experience) which is enough time to really get to know a place and bond with other people that you're with. Also, for people that are a bit shy, and who wouldn't like the "forwardness" of meeting people in a hostel dorm, a work-away experience can provide a really nice environment to meet new people in a calmer way.

It's a great chance to learn new skills! My partner once stayed with a family that taught him glass-blowing. How cool is that?!"

Look for workaway options at workaway.info or wwoof.net

I'll end this chapter with a story by my friend, Lisa, who traveled on a budget. She paid it forward to me years later, when I came and stayed with her in Scotland. The travel world is full of beautiful, heartwarming connections like this.

"I had been studying abroad for a semester in Scotland, and many other Americans were doing the same. A few of us decided to travel around Europe a bit after term before going home for Christmas. I didn't have the same amount of time or money as the others, so I decided to meet them in Paris instead of joining for the full trip. I really had no idea what I was doing. One of the other students said she'd plan everything, so I just needed to book my plane ticket. So that's all I did! My friends would meet me at the airport when I arrived, and that was the plan.

My first lesson was that budget airlines in Europe don't tend to fly to the main city airports - a flight to 'Paris' was actually a flight to Beauvais! Again, not having traveled much, especially by plane, I didn't really notice anything strange when booking the ticket. We landed around midnight, went through customs, and everyone else from the flight filed to a bus. I just stood there, looking around an empty airport - my friends nowhere in sight, but I wasn't' worried. They were going to meet me, so I waited outside and watched the bus drive away.

It was only when the airport closed, and they locked up the doors, that I started to worry. A security guard walked up to me and asked what I was doing, and I think I burst into tears. I managed to explain I was meeting my friends, and he just looked around and said, well, they're not here, so you'll need to leave. Luckily, a savvy taxi driver was still lurking around, and somehow it was agreed that I would stay at a hotel in Beauvais and try to find my friends in the morning. The taxi driver drove me to a hotel, and I checked in. I had no idea what time it was, but it was late, and I couldn't figure out how to work the heater in the room, so I was freezing. I turned on the TV and found an American football game being dubbed over in French - it was very surreal! So, wrapped up in all my clothes and watching football, I fell asleep, not having a clue where I was.

It was a nice morning, and I left the hotel with a plan - find an internet cafe and information about the hotel where my friends were staying (which had been emailed to me), call them, and figure out how to get to them. As I wandered through the town, I noticed a police station. I figured they could help me, so I wandered in.

At this point, I should add, I don't speak French. At all. And neither of the two police officers at the front desk spoke English. In mixed Spanish and English, trying to explain that I needed to get in touch with my friends. Soon, all five officers on duty were in the front office, deciphering my story.

Two officers agreed to take me to an internet cafe to get online, so we jumped in the car. To date, this is still my only journey in the back of a police car.

As we drove through the little town, one officer turned around and asked me, "Have you met Pierre Noel?" I said I hadn't, and he pulled over the car and rolled down my window to a man dressed as Santa Claus, shouting, "We have an American in the back!" Pierre Noel threw me some candy, wished me a Merry Christmas, and we went along our merry way.

We came to a job center, and in hindsight, I can only imagine what the staff was thinking when two police officers walked in, escorting a wide-eyed American! But I got online, printed off the hotel information, and they drove me back to the station where they phoned the hotel for me. It rang through to my friends' room, and although the officers couldn't understand what I was saying, I know they saw the change in my facial expression because they all burst into grins as I chattered away to my friend and figured out how to find them in Paris. I hung up, and the officers took me to a train station.

I think one of the officers actually paid for my ticket to Paris, and they waited with me on the platform to make sure I got on the right train. I had a really peaceful train journey through the French countryside before reuniting with my friends in Paris' city center." - Lisa, USA

# Chapter 4

## Traveling Alone

*"I'd rather go by myself than not go at all."*

- Me

One Halloween, while in Japan, I was feeling incredibly lonely. Whenever I felt this kind of loneliness, there was one place I could go that would lift my spirits. It was one of the first things I sought out when I arrived in the country. A Tex-Mex Restaurant. Nothing like Enchiladas, Margaritas, and chips and salsa to bring me comfort when I was feeling homesick. It's also where I could meet other guacamole-deprived Americans who were desperate for a bit of tortilla and Mariachi.

I walked into a full restaurant of people dressed up in Halloween costumes. The restaurant was usually full of foreigners, but this time, it was full of the locals all dressed up in their Halloween attire. I tried to hide in the corner, where I could see everyone and stay out of the way, but as always in my life, I stood out. A table full of vampires and vampirettes noticed me almost right away.

I tried to pretend like I didn't notice their blatant pointing and staring, but my sense of humor got the best of me, and I giggled and waved. They waved back, excited I was interacting. Just as one of them was about to get up to talk to me, another person approached my table.

"Are you alone?" someone said. "Please, join us at our table." She was dressed as a witch and turned out to be a 68-year-old Grandma. She wanted me to join her and her friends to drink and talk with them. Of course, I said yes, and the next thing I knew, I was talking and partying the night away with these friendly ladies. At times, the conversation had me laughing so hard I had tears running down my face. They kept ordering me margaritas and, in the end, paid for my meal and drinks.

It was a wonderful night, and I went home drunk, less lonely, with a hovering hangover, and another good story.

## Solo Travel

My first solo travel experience was in New York. I booked my first hostel, near Times Square, and I toured the city alone. I'll admit, there were times when I got a little scared, but I stayed on the well-beaten path, clung on to my purse, and made sure I knew how to get back before I went anywhere. I rode away from New York, satisfied with what I had seen and proud of myself.

## A Time for Reflection

Traveling alone teaches you to enjoy your own company. Earlier in the book, I mentioned spontaneously booking a trip to Europe. I'd gone through something that broke my heart and completely crushed my spirit. I was in such a state of darkness. I decided to buy a one-way ticket to Europe and travel around for a while, and I ended up being gone for about four and a half months. In the beginning, being alone was difficult. I had so many thoughts and feelings that I'd shoved aside, and they kept coming back up. So many things that I needed to sort through.

During that trip, I had very little money, and tried to take any kind of shortcut that I could. I constantly took buses, because they were so much cheaper than flights and trains. Unfortunately, the trips were long. The longest bus ride that I took was about 16 hours. I wouldn't say I liked it at first, but I found myself loving these hours over time. I would read, think, and sort out messy thoughts and emotions, and almost always felt a little bit better when I arrived at my new destination.

I was about three months into my trip when I realized that I was okay again. I still had mending to do, but the journey and spending so much time alone had sped up the healing process. This is one of the main reasons I choose to travel alone. Here is a status I wrote about it during my trip:

"Traveling alone generally means facing an entire range of emotions, from complete and utter joy to heartbreaking pain. It all comes up. You are depending on yourself to meet your physical, mental, emotional, and social needs. There is so much good that comes from doing this. I believe that everyone should do it, even if it means just taking a weekend and going outdoors or visiting a town nearby. So many questions get answered. So many hurts get explained. So many joyous things happen. So many moments of peace happen.

There are times when I'm so thankful to be alone. When I'm hungry, lost, when I need to think, when I want to read, or when I'm moody. However, there are moments I wish someone were here. I told some girls that I met the other night that I had cried earlier that day, and one of the girls I met pulled me aside and thanked me for sharing because she feels that way too sometimes. She feels like she is supposed to be happy and cheerful all the time because she's having the experience of a lifetime. But when you are alone all the time, like we are, it's impossible to keep up a cheerful façade. It really forces you to face yourself and the things you don't want to face. A good portion of why I'm traveling for this long by myself is for this reason."

## Meet New People

Although I spend more time alone than I normally would at home, I still meet many people while traveling. When you meet people traveling, no matter the age or gender, something really cool happens. You feel like you've known the person for a long time. There is no pressure to make a long-lasting friendship.

You know you will likely never see the person again, so you don't have the standard barriers that go up with people you meet at home. You bond over being travelers, you bond over things you've seen and will see, you bond over the crazy experiences you have together, and you bond in the present. I've had this with countless travelers, and every single one of them has a special place in my heart.

When you meet another traveler, you often find yourself spending time with them while you are still together. Most times, I've spent a day with someone before one or both of us needed to leave. For most, I assume I will never see them again, but we all know that the possibility of meeting again someday is there. I've met back up with a few in different parts of the world, and we pick up right where we left off.

## Other Advantages of Traveling Alone

- If I am traveling with others, there tends to be more stress and planning involved. When I'm alone, I never have to worry about what someone else wants to see or do; I simply take it one day at a time and see where the days take me. Traveling with others means making sure everyone gets to experience and see what they want, which can be rather tiring, trying to make it all work.

- I eat whatever I want. This is a big deal – trust me. It is a sad day when I am craving something, but no one else wants it. Maybe I want Gelato for the 4th time that day. When I'm alone, there is no one there to say, "Again?!" I just stop and eat it.

- I set the pace. I never have to worry about someone who wants to stare at a painting for 20 minutes or, in turn, someone who gets restless when I decide to people-watch from a park bench for 30 minutes.

- I go wherever I want to go.

- How I spend my time is my choice. I can sleep-in as late as I want, or wake up as early as I want. I like to sleep in, which tends to be a problem if the person I am traveling with is ready to go at 7 am.

- It is a lot less stressful. If I am lost, no big deal. If I didn't see everything I hoped to see, no big deal. If I am feeling tired or grumpy, no big deal. If you're traveling with someone else, depending on the person you're with, these things will be a big deal.

# Booking the Trip

# Chapter 5

## Where Should I Go?

*"No expectations. It's never like what you expect it will be."*

-Laura, Germany

When I was about 25, I decided I desperately wanted to see Europe. I carefully looked up different options and found a cruise that went to about four countries I wanted to see. I had one friend going with me, and we were both pretty excited - until one sleepless night when I started researching ways to see more countries for the same price.

The more I searched, the more the internet told me that I should consider backpacking instead. It was kind of a scary thought; I'd never been to Europe before, and I felt like my lack of knowledge would make it very difficult to get around. After days of searching, I brought all of my newfound wisdom about backpacking Europe to my friend. She was extremely hesitant until I started telling her the benefits, such as only spending about half the amount we'd planned, seeing double the amount of places, and seeing so much more of each country, and so on. The more I talked, the more she started to agree, and the next thing we knew, we were on our way to travel through eight countries in two and a half weeks.

It was a whirlwind of a trip, but each day was so compact with seeing beautiful places, meeting incredible people, and experiencing new adventures. It was more than we could have ever hoped for, and it set us both on a life of travel from that point on.

## What kind of trip are you looking for?

Two different scenarios:

1. You are on a beach somewhere beautiful. You are staying in a gorgeous resort, you have a Mai Tai in one hand, an incredible book in the other, and you are relaxed. You've been doing the same thing for the past three days, and have plans to do it for three more days until you have to head back to reality. You are in heaven.

2. You are in a tiny restaurant in Seoul, Korea. You have just made friends with the Korean group at the table next to you, and they want to buy you a drink. You spend the rest of the night talking with them, and they invite you to karaoke with them. The evening ends with trying all kinds of new foods and drinks, and it turns out to be an incredible night.

One is a vacation, and the other is a traveling experience.

| Traveling Experience | Vacation |
| --- | --- |
| You seek to learn more about the culture | You seek to see tourist attractionsthat may, or may not represent the real culture of the destination |
| You travel for as long as possible, sacrificing the "finer" things in the process | You travel for as long as you can afford to travel, and tend to spend more than you planned |
| You get to know new people from around the world | You get closer to the people you are on vacation with |
| You seek opportunities to get to know more about the culture you are in. | You seek opportunities to relax and enjoy the environment you are in |
| Save money so you can travel longer | Often spending more than you planned |

Vacationers tend to be somewhere for one of four reasons:

1. To get pictures

2. To relax

3. To party

4. To spend time with friends or family doing one of the above three things.

Traveling experiences are more hardcore. People looking for this tend to go from one place to the next without much of a plan most times. They go into a destination respectfully, and try to blend in with the culture around them, however difficult that may be. They seek local restaurants and experiences and try to be as open as possible as they learn about the place they are in and the people around them. They are open to major tourist attractions, but they also seek smaller experiences that others would likely overlook. For example, dinner with a local family may not seem like a big deal to the average person, but it is a HUGE deal for someone seeking authentic traveling experiences.

Travelers still party, seek opportunities to relax, and take lots of pictures, but these are not the primary reasons for the trips. They know they can do the same things at home and try to get more out of their trip. Something I like to call "Traveler's High" comes over them, and suddenly, they see the world around them through new lenses. A few things happen when this "high" hits:

- You realize how small you are and how much you don't know

- You CRAVE cultural knowledge on a level you didn't even know existed

- You hang onto the present with an iron grip

- You realize you can't take that "high" home with you, and there is a grieving period when you return home.

- You often find yourself returning home with a new appreciation for small gifts, such as hot showers, current relationships, and a big warm bed.

- You will never be the same again.

Both types of trips have value and can offer peace and restoration to your soul. I find myself craving traveling experiences more often, but there are times I simply need a relaxing and fun vacation.

*"Whether you are on vacation or traveling around for a while, you're always a tourist to locals."*

- Jon, Switzerland

My friend Jon makes an excellent point. No matter how respectful you are, how long you've been in a certain place, or who you hang out with while traveling, you will always be considered a tourist to the locals.

*"Before I plan a trip, I think about my expectations for the trip. Do I want to relax? Do I want to explore with the locals? Or do I want to*

*hit all of the tourist attractions? I also make sure to align these expectations with my travel companions. This helps limit disagreements on what activities to do on our trip."*

-Ebony, USA

## Where Should I Go?

What a wonderful question. The possibilities are endless. What do you want to experience? Here are some ideas and personal experiences that I have had the pleasure of taking within them. If you are a new traveler go someplace that is familiar to you. For a lot of people from the USA, that means Europe. Places like Ireland or Scotland are popular destinations because they are relatively close, the people speak the same language, and it is very easy to get around.

Stunning Beaches

San Blas Islands in Panama and Gili Air in Indonesia tie for my favorite islands. Both were exactly what you see when you picture exotic islands. The sand was pure white, the ocean a gorgeous turquoise, and both places had a limited amount of people on them.

In the San Blas Islands, the indigenous people of that area run the islands and their story is inspiring. They are some of the few indigenous people that were able to fight off the Spaniards and keep their land. The islands are some of the most beautiful you will ever see, and in order to see them, you need to book a tour. The lodgings are modest at best. I opted to stay on an island with huts. The sand was the floor, and our beds were cots with mosquito nets around them. It felt a bit like camping, but with a bed. The island was so small it only took about 10 minutes to walk around it. It offered a swing, some hammocks, and a place to gather for food. My tour provided three meals, hotel pick-up, two night's stay, two days of island hopping and a guided tour through one of the water villages. If you are a luxury traveler, I wouldn't recommend these islands. However, if you love the outdoors and don't mind "roughing it" a little, this tour is perfect. If visiting the San Blas Islands is something that interests you, you need to book fast. The islands are rapidly disappearing due to rising water levels, and my tour guide said it was estimated that the islands would all be gone in less than 20 years.

Gili Air was a spontaneous decision. I was in Lombok, Indonesia, and I had just spent four days incredibly sick. I was more than ready to move on when I noticed several signs that advertised the Gili Islands. Intrigued, I asked my server some questions and booked a trip within the hour. The next day, I found myself pulling up on a boat onto the stunning white shores of Gili Air. Like the San Blas Islands, pictures don't do it justice.

Each of the three Gili Islands has its own reputation. Gili Trawangan is known to be the best for singles looking to party, Gili Meno is the getaway for romantic couples, and I chose Gili Air because it was rumored to be relaxing. I wasn't disappointed. I spent the days snorkeling and getting cheap massages. My nights were spent relaxing with a drink in hand at the restaurants. While I was there, I stayed in a hostel, but there are several gorgeous hotel options for those who prefer them. These hotels are much cheaper than standard beach hotels. They are not as lavish as resorts, but you can expect great service and gorgeous views if you don't mind a simple hotel room.

Why Beaches?

- The beauty!

- The smell of saltwater

- Relaxation: Whether you tan or like to lay in the shade, the beach is an excellent time to catch up on reading, thoughts, or to simply do nothing.

- Adventure: When people think of beaches, they often think of lying around, but there are a ton of things to try on the water, such as snorkeling, diving, paddle boarding, surfing, kayaking, the list goes on and on.

- Fun beach drinks; Mai Tais, Margaritas, Pina Coladas

## Jungle Adventures

Jungles are badass, and every inch of what you can see holds life, beauty, and danger. One of my favorite experiences in jungles was in the Peruvian Amazon. I was on a trip with five of my closest girlfriends, and we had just hiked Machu Picchu and decided to go to the Amazon as well. We took a three-night tour with a guide, who was indigenous to the area, and she stayed with us throughout. Our tour included all meals, several excursions, and one night of Caiman hunting. Our lodging had a screen opening at the top, and we were able to see and smell the world around us as we slept. The electricity was on a generator and only worked for about two hours every night. Within those two hours, we ate and settled into our beds before losing power around 9 pm.

There were giant insects everywhere that both terrified and fascinated us, and although none of us did well with insects, we all adapted quickly to having them around. I wasn't even fazed when a huge cockroach crawled out of my backpack once, something that would have typically made me scream.

The best part of the whole trip was Caiman hunting. Caimans are similar to crocodiles, and the object of our excursion was to row our canoe as close as we could get to them. The stars were brighter than I'd ever seen, and we could clearly see the milky way and the southern constellations. We found several Caiman and were both scared and amused to see how close the guides got to them. I could reach out and touch a few of them. A little too cozy for my liking.

## Why Jungles?

- Enormous Flowers: sometimes bigger than your head!

- Clean Air: It smells so fresh.

- Plant Life: I wouldn't recommend touching anything in the jungle, but just looking at the multitude of plant life around you is enough to feel enveloped by nature.

- Birds: All kinds of birds fill the sky and trees. You can hear them singing to each other as they go about their day.

- Medicine: If you get the right tour, you will learn about the origin of modern medicine as they show you which plants heal and which plants are deadly.

- Monkeys: I'm not a huge fan of monkeys - they are sneaky, diseased ridden, and thieves, but the world loves them.

- Adventure: Even a simple boat ride offers adventure. The jungle is wild and stunning, and you can't help but feel a little adrenalin rush as you explore it.

- Other kinds of animals, plant life, and insects: You'll see all sorts of things, some that you would probably prefer to miss, and others that you will feel so lucky to have witnessed.

## Hiking

I seek out hiking opportunities on most of my trips. Usually, I look for hiking trails as a way to get out of whatever city I'm in, but a few of my travels have been completely centered around a hike. Trolltunga was one of them. Trolltunga is a famous rock in Norway that juts out like a plank over the stunning view of Lake Ringedalsvatnet.

The first time I ever saw the view in a picture, I knew I had to go. I flew into Bergan, Norway, which is a cute harbor town in the summertime. The sunlight hours were 23 hours and 8 minutes of the day, leaving the city in darkness for only 52 minutes. I took a bus to Odda, found my hostel, and took a shuttle to the trailhead. I was alone for the hike, but several people were on the path, so I was never really alone. From the beginning to the end of the hike to Trolltunga, the views were breathtaking! Over and over again, I found myself gasping in awe. Everything, everywhere, was SO beautiful. Another bonus of the hike is that there were several creeks with water along the way, and it was safe enough to drink.

The only slight disappointment was getting to Trolltunga itself. The view was stunning, but there was an hour-long line to get the iconic picture. I decided it was worth it because I had nothing to do when I got back but sleep in an empty hostel, so I stood in line and made friends with the people around me. We all helped each other get photos. Afterward, I found a little more secluded place, ate my lunch, and just took in the view.

## Why Hiking?

- Offers unique views of the area.

- Allows you to be with locals.

- Hiking is always an accomplishment, and it feels good to be outside enjoying the local scenery.

- A great way to exercise if you've been eating, drinking, and relaxing more than usual.

- Free form of exercise for those who like to work out often.

- Hiking can be slightly different in other countries. For example, in China, there are restaurants and stalls along the way. You can stop to enjoy a boiled egg, beer, and even meals as you get to the top.

## Stunning Mountains

Nothing brings peace to my soul like a stunning view of mountains. You can reach these places by backpacking, cable cars, hiking, driving, or trains. Some of the sites are easy to access, such as Interlaken, Switzerland or Hallstatt, Austria but for other, you have to work harder to enjoy. There are climbing communities at the top of mountains worldwide, so if you love to backpack and camp in the wilderness, you will find these opportunities with internet searches, or even better, if you show up and ask locals.

When I was on one of my longer trips, I had hit a point of traveling numbness that had me less joyful to see some of the cities I was visiting. I needed a break. I was in Krakow, Poland, and I knew I wanted to see Budapest, Hungary, but I decided to research hiking in Slovakia since it was on the way. I found a small town called Poprad. When I arrived a couple of days later, I was not disappointed. Not only did the nearby mountains provide a gorgeous and reviving hike, but the town itself turned out to be exactly what I needed. It had an affordable Spa behind the hotels with bathing pools, it had healthy food options, and of course, I met some great people that made my time in the little town perfect.

## Why Mountains?

- There are multiple ways to exercise! You can run, bike, ski, walk, or climb.

- Fresh Air: I'm convinced that pure mountain air heals the body of many kinds of physical and emotional aches

- The peaceful feeling of being in nature

- Learning about the rocks and landscapes of the area as a hands-on geology lesson

- Camping: If you love to sleep outside in nature, the experience of waking up in the middle of the mountains is unparalleled. Camping experiences can be found worldwide for those who crave the outdoors but prefer a more comfortable sleeping arrangement.

- The quiet (depending on where you go)

## Ancient Ruins

Standing in front of a ruin is such a humbling experience. I love to think about the history as I look at them. I picture what it must have looked like, I think about the labor it took to build it, I wonder about the people who lived in it, and I consider how quickly even the most powerful people and places can tumble. There are so many untold stories in these places. The true events have been bent and lost overtime no matter how hard historians have tried to hang on to it. So many inspirational events of things have happened and will never be told. So many ancient peoples came to their own revolutions of happiness, love, hate, fear, and family.

Machu Picchu is highly commercialized and trendy to visit these days, so when I opted to take a three-day hiking tour to reach it, I was expecting the atmosphere to be polluted with a touristy vibe. We hiked up early in the morning to watch the sunrise, and I'll never forget the moment the sun hit the ruins. It was magic. There were six of us standing together, but none could speak. Everything in me paused - my thoughts, my aching limbs, my ever-present sense of anxiety, and I'm even sure my breathing stopped. I'll never forget that moment.

## Why Ruins?

- For the love and importance of history

- To learn about different cultures

- To remind yourself that life is precious

- To recall the joy of modern-day conveniences

- To see the evidence of life that you've only seen in textbooks

## Bustling Cities

When I'm outside in nature, it's easier to reflect and find peace. When I'm in a city, I find myself getting swept up in the hustle and bustle, and peace takes a bit more effort. This is why I've often sought out city parks as a place of refuge so I can rejuvenate. Even so, I love cities. The creativity of humanity is on display everywhere you look, and often in ways that you'd have never imagined seeing it. Street performers, architecture, famous buildings and structures, street vendors, art, fashion, storefronts, restaurants, transportation and education are just points in an inexhaustible list.

My favorite cities include local culture, convenient food and entertainment sources, walkability, and an upbeat atmosphere. Some of my favorite cities are Budapest, Hungary; Hanoi, Vietnam; Tokyo, Japan; and Medellin, Colombia. It's always amazing to me when a culture can figure out how to incorporate tourism. There are so many cities that seem to have only one or the other.

Culture is most often shoved to the side and hidden from tourists which is understandable, but it's less personable that way. Shanghai is a good example of this. There are glitzy shopping streets and stunning views of the city, but it isn't until you walk a few blocks over that you see bits of the real culture- tons of street carts selling all kinds of items spread about the streets. When I was there, street carts were illegal, so at one point, I was trying to buy some food, and everyone in the area started yelling and packing up as quickly as they could. In less than a minute, all those beautiful people and their carts were gone. For me, the best cities mix it all together so you can mingle with the culture as you enjoy the experience.

Why Cities?

- Often hold the most beloved and popular tourist activities. Hard to do pub crawls and ghost tours in the mountains.

- Famous structures and buildings such as towers or cathedrals

- Museums

- Cities are easy to reach.

- Food - holy moly, the food. If nothing else convinces you to visit cities around the world, the food should. Each culture has their delicacies and specialties, and it is such an honor and privilege to walk into a restaurant and get served the local cuisine.

- Easy access to shops, grocery stores, and restaurants

## Backpacking Routes

There are backpacking routes all over the internet. Where do you want to go? There is likely a backpacker's trail for you. You'll find all sorts of tips and tricks to help you get from point A to point B on these routes. People will recommend different ways of transportation, places to eat, places to sleep, and things to see along the way. Here are popular ones:

**The Banana Pancake Trail** in South East Asia. It takes you to places like Thailand, Cambodia, Laos, Vietnam, Malaysia,

Indonesia, Philippines, or Singapore. And yes, Banana Pancakes are as amazing as they sound.

**The Gringo Trails** in Central and South America. It takes you to places like Colombia, Ecuador, Peru, Bolivia, Brazil, Argentina, or Chile. Or it takes you to places like Mexico, Guatemala, Belize, Costa Rica, or Panama.

**Backpacking in Europe** throughout Europe. There is not set trail, but you'll find information for any route you are looking for on the internet. You'll find a ton of information, easily, because almost any kind of route has been done and recorded.

**Backpacking elsewhere**-Just like in Europe, you will find routes for regions such as Asia, Northern Africa, Southern Africa, The Silk Road, and so on. These routes are not as popular, but you will still find tons of information from previous travelers.

For more route ideas, I'd suggest going to wikivoyage.org/wiki/itineraries

# Chapter 6

## Booking the Flight

*"Try searching for flights in Incognito mode; you might be able to find cheaper flights. Also, look up the best times to buy tickets. I've heard it's 1 am."*

- Farrah, Kuwait

I had just spent two amazing weeks at a Spanish School in a tiny mountain town in Colombia called San Carlos. Thanks to noisy and admittedly fun roommates, I got very little sleep on my last night. I got on a bus from San Carlos to Medellin, and the plan was to get to the bus station and then take a taxi to the airport to catch my 3:05 pm flight. As we were arriving in Medellin, I noticed that we were really close to the airport. I also realized I could save myself a ton of money by just getting a taxi from the next stop rather than going all the way to the bus station. Brilliant, right?

It would have been if I had not been in such a hurry to get off the bus and into the available taxi. I left my bag on the bus. This bag had clothing, my laptop, and a ton of other stuff I REALLY did not want to lose. This did not occur to me until I was about two minutes into the taxicab that I shared with three other people. I panicked and suddenly started cussing, "SHIT SHIT SHIT SHIT!!" Everyone was staring at me in alarm as I freaked out and tried to explain in terrible Spanish that I'd left my 'Bolsa' on the bus.

It was a mess. After a TON of hilarious phone conversations, I ended up having to take a taxi to the bus station to retrieve my bag. I was relieved to find my bag but concerned about missing my flight. It was then that I looked at the flight details again. OH NO. It didn't say 3:05 pm. It said 13:05 pm, which meant I had already missed my flight. At this point, all I could do was laugh. At least I had my bag.

As most blunder stories almost always do, the situation turned out fine, and I found a flight for later on that night for about $60.00.

## Searching for Flight Deals

Once upon a time, I had no idea how to search for flight deals. I desperately wanted to see London, and summer was the only time I could. So I booked the round trip tickets from Phoenix to London for $1200.00. OUCH!

I look back on that now and flinch. I can't believe I ever spent that kind of money on a plane ticket. The problem was, London was my focus, and I HAD to see it. I had tunnel vision. All I could see was London during that one week in June. My options were so limited that I had no choice but to pay the fee.

Tunnel vision is one of the biggest deterrents to travelers. They are so focused on seeing the ONE place they want to see that they miss opportunities and deals that could be close to their chosen destination.

Let's say you long to see Rome. You have time off around Thanksgiving and are looking up plane tickets to Rome around that time. You check the price, and it is around $1500.00.- way too expensive. This is where so many travelers give up.

But what you don't know is that there are 400USD tickets to other destinations around the world at the same time. You might even be able to fly to Milan for 800 dollars less and take a train to Rome. Not only do you save money on this route, but you allow yourself the opportunity to see more.

When people think of booking flights, they think of the more traditional route, which is searching for the time and the place in one search. Nowadays, most flight search engines will allow you to be more flexible with your inquiries, and it could save you hundreds of dollars.

Here are the four ways you can search for your flights:

1. **Search by the date you want to leave:** Searching by the time you are able to go but being open to different locations.

2. **Search by location you want to see:** Search by a specific place you want to see but on a flexible time table.

3. **Having no specific location or date:** Choosing a location based on flight deals and experience.

4. **Search by exact location and date:** Choosing the exact place you want to see and the exact time you are able to go.

Let's talk about the four ways to book a flight in order from the priciest to the cheapest.

## Specific Time and Location

If money isn't an issue, this is the fastest and easiest way to travel. Your transitions are likely to be smoother, your layovers will be a little shorter and your overall travel time will be quicker. There are exceptions; I've been able to save time by booking one leg of the trip separately, but if you would prefer it simple, this is the way to go.

If you are trying to save money, but this is really the only way you'd be willing to travel, there are a few things you can do.

- Search by destination and see if it is cheaper to fly in a day early or a day later.

- Don't buy the tickets right away. Set a "watch fare" on a website that will allow it, and it will notify you when the flight dips below a certain price.

## Specific Time with Flexible Location

This image demonstrates a Google flight search with an open destination. You'll click on "Explore Destination," and you'll be able to search whatever region you are hoping for by moving around on the map. This is an example of some great flight deals from Phoenix to some major European cities.

Instead of choosing a specific destination. Put the city you will fly out of but leave the "Where to" blank. Look for the words "More Destinations" or "Explore Destinations." When you choose "More Destinations," a map will pop up and will give you several options around the world. Select a general location, such as Europe, to see prices listed all over Europe. You'll see major city names along with the prices. You can select one of these places to see airlines and times.

**Click on "Explore Destinations" to find a price-map.**
This option only shows on a desktop. It won't show up for a mobile app.

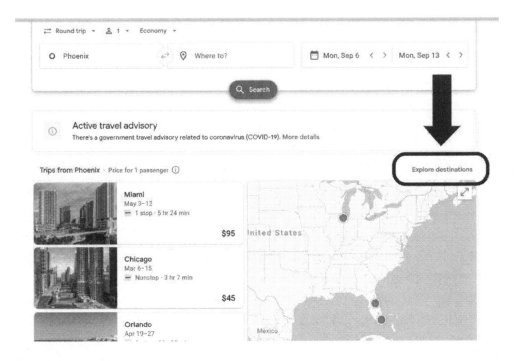

Scroll around on the map to see prices around the world for the dates you selected.

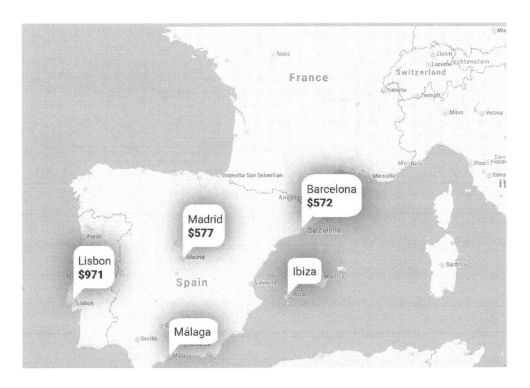

## Specific Location with Flexible Time

Another great way to save money is by choosing a destination in your search and then checking multiple dates for the cheapest rates. This image is an example of a flight from Phoenix to Paris. This is for the entire month of October, but the search will allow me to view rates over the course of several months. You can see here that the cheapest time to fly from Phoenix to Paris is on Oct 16th. If you had gone forward a few months, you might have found even better deals for this route.

**Click here.** A calendar and the amounts for each date will pop up.

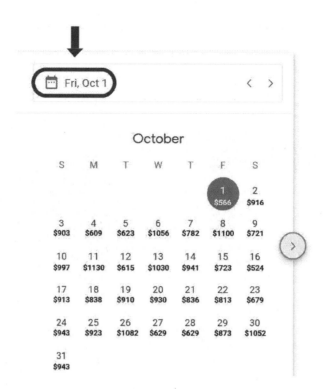

## Flexible Time and Location

Being flexible is a great position to be in. "Where can I go for $400?" There is no doubt you'll be able to find a cheap flight; it's just a matter of finding and getting it booked. When you are in this position, I'd recommend searching by a specific time and leaving your destination open to search for deals. If you don't find a location you want to visit, change the date and search again. This way, you can see the many options available. Google will even let you search by month. Say you want to travel in April sometime. You let google know you plan to travel in April and it will give the prices to many suggested routes out of your city within the month of April.

Just be aware that this method leaves the most room for procrastination, and not getting anything booked. You are more likely to feel conflicted over multiple locations and never come to a decision. If this happens, choose the one that calls to you more, and remember there is always a next time for the other competing places in your mind.

## Ways to Narrow Down Destinations

You've found some great places but which one to choose?!

- If you are on a budget, you can also research how expensive the country is and choose the cheapest one to eat, stay, and get around.

- Toss a coin!

- Choose a creative way to choose a place: For example, you can invite some friends to play a game, each of them representing an eligible destination. Carl represents Japan. Shannon represents Colombia. Whoever wins the game is where you go!

- If you know a traveler, ask them for their opinion. Even if they have not been to a certain location, they will likely be able to tell you which they would prefer and why.

## Extra Tips and Suggestions

- Use a major hub and search deals from there. You can save yourself hundreds of dollars by merely booking a leg of the trip separately. I live in Phoenix, so I book most international flights out of Los Angeles (LA) and book a separate ticket from Phoenix to LA. This typically saves me a few hundred dollars.

- Research budget airlines for the area you want to visit. They aren't always on major search engines.

- Travel with a carry-on if possible. In the U.S., more and more are charging for carry-on, but in foreign countries, it is still cheaper. Plus, it's really nice not to be lugging around huge bags. As my friend Steve says, "BUDGET FLIGHTS CAN BE MORE EXPENSIVE THAN NORMAL FLIGHTS IF YOU CHECK BAGS"

- Look up travel credit cards for points. I still have a lot to learn about using airline points, but I did recently take 6 flights around Central and South America without paying a dime. The only exception was missing a flight and having to pay $60 for a new ticket.

## Websites that Can Help Save Money

- **Scott's Cheap Flights:** You'll pay an annual fee, but it will pay for itself if you find a deal. You supply information on which airports you want to see deals out of, and it will send you phenomenal deals every day. This is my favorite one to use. https://scottscheapflights.com/

- **Google Flights:** I search for the majority of my flights using Google Flights. It has the most options for searching and finding deals. https://www.google.com/flights

- **Skyscanner:** This is also a good one to search for deals; just be aware that taxes and fees are not always included in the first price. https://www.skyscanner.com/

- **Airfare Watchdog:** It allows you to keep track of price drops for specific routes. https://www.airfarewatchdog.com/

# Chapter 7

## Lodging

*"Try to get in touch with other travelers; they often have good advice for hostels, spots you should see, hidden places, and good restaurants."*

- Manuel, Germany

I was in Munich, Germany, for Oktoberfest when I rented a room on Airbnb. The owner was also there, in her own room, and we shared a bathroom.

On my first day at Oktoberfest, I learned the hard way that the beer was not watered down as I had expected. I drank two heaping mugs full of beer and was flat out drunk. I made my way back to the apartment in the early afternoon for a nap and stopped to use the restroom. As I was making my way in, I lost my balance and FELL RIGHT INTO the tub. The shower curtain wrapped itself around me, and it was a bit of a struggle to get myself out of the tub again in my Dirndl and drunken state. I finished up and passed out, not thinking much of it.

Two days later, the owner texted, "What happened to the soap dispenser?!" I had no idea what she was talking about, and it wasn't until several hours and one beer later that I suddenly remembered falling in the tub. I realized that I'd probably broken it when I fell in. Luckily, she had a good sense of humor and was not upset by it. She said, "I had a feeling something happened after the Oktoberfest beer!" She also mentioned the curtain rod was completely crooked, and she had to straighten it back out again! Talk about embarrassing!

When you are searching for lodging, these are the qualities to look for in a room:

- Safety

- Location

- Cleanliness

- Comfort

## Hostels
**Q: Is it even worth going if I have to share a room with strangers?**
**A: Yes**
When people think of hostels, they generally think of dingy rooms that smell bad, some guy snoring, dirty accommodations, and the movie "Taken." I've stayed in over 100 hostels, and only about 10% were this way (minus the Taken part). When I travel, especially if I'm alone, I almost always stay in hostels. When I started staying in hostels, the only reason I chose them was because they saved me

money. Now I stay in them for many reasons, and I recommend them to anyone who isn't a luxury traveler.

## Meeting People

Hostels are the best way to meet other travelers. You meet friendly and open-minded people from around the world. Hostels often have happy hours, put on city tours, serve meals, and include classes designed to help strangers meet. Their ratings depend on people enjoying the atmosphere, so the best ones go out of their way to make sure you have a good time and meet new people while you stay there.

## Safety

I use a website called *www.hostelworld.com* to book hostels, which rates the location, safety, cleanliness, atmosphere, and more. If I'm in a country that is known to be dangerous for women, hostels are the safest way for me to sleep. I feel a lot safer in a room full of people than in a hotel room by myself. If bad people knew I was alone in a hotel, anything could happen without many knowing it. In a hostel, several people would hear and wake up if something was happening to me. I always make sure there are lockers in hostels, and I bring my own lock in case I need it. For females, most hostels offer "Female Only" dorm rooms.

PLEASE: DO NOT CHOOSE A DODGY HOTEL over a hostel that has a good safety rating.

## Age

Hostels are primarily used by travelers in their 20's, but I see people of all ages in them. There are usually some people over the age of 40. I once saw a couple that had to be in their late 70's. They were watching all the "kids" play beer pong and laughing along with everyone. If you are "older," search for the words "quiet" in the reviews and avoid the hostels that say, "Party hostel" or "loud."

## Private Rooms

Some hostels offer private rooms as well. They can be just as expensive as regular hotels but often, they are still much cheaper. If I can justify the price, I often choose these rooms because I'd have my own space with all the benefits of staying at a hostel.

## Amenities

Typically, hostels have their own kitchens, so you can make your food instead of spending a ton of money eating out. Once, I was at a hostel in Scotland and the entire block got shut down by the police. I was so hungry, but I wasn't allowed to leave. I said as much to the family next to me and the parents offered to share the food that they were planning to cook. I had a lovely meal with them.

Hostels can be creative with their common rooms. I've seen hammocks, swings, cute porches, bars with amazing happy hour prices, movie rooms, gardens, and more. These common rooms allow you to meet other people, work on your computer, or participate in group activities. I'll be honest; you never know what you will get in terms of shared bathrooms. Most are nice, but some, well, READ THE REVIEWS!

## Location

Hostels are typically located in the best areas. You'd be spending hundreds of dollars to stay in some of these incredible locations at other lodgings. Check the location rating for details, but you'll easily find hostels right in the middle of all the things you want to see and do.

## Sleep

I never sleep well on my first night in a room full of strangers. Part of this is because I've spent most of my adult life single, and the other part is getting used to the new settings. On the second and third nights, I sleep fine. You'll adjust quickly and sharing a room with others won't seem like a big deal after the first night. Earplugs, headphones, eye masks, a towel hung from the bars - all these things can help you adapt and sleep.

## Price
Hostels are typically between $10 - $25 a night.

## Airbnb
Airbnb's are a great way to experience a new place. Most Airbnb's are homes, condos, or living spaces, but there are some really creative options as well, such as tents, RVs, or Yurts. You can find them in great locations, and they generally come with a kitchen if you are hoping to cook some meals at home. For a lot of people, they prefer Airbnb's over hotels because they are cozy and accommodate more people. I don't prefer them, to be honest, I don't like being in someone's home and possibly… oh I don't know, falling into a shower fully clothed and breaking a soap dispenser. Being in someone's home makes me uncomfortable, but I've done it many times and would still recommend it for families and friends traveling together.

## Renting an Entire Place
Renting an entire place is the most preferred way to use Airbnb. You get the whole space to yourself, and it can be nice to have a little home to go back to after a day of touring. Pay attention to the ratings and reviews - previous guests will give you an idea of what the stay is like.

## Renting Out a Room

Renting a room is a more economical way of using Airbnb. You'll rent out a private room rather than an entire place, and the hosts will generally be in the home with you. Most come with a private bathroom, but in some places, you share that as well. You'll want to read the description and reviews carefully with this method. Some hosts create a Bed and Breakfast feel and will want to have a meal or two with you. Others will generally stay out of your way, and you may not see them the entire stay.

## Things to Remember

One important thing to remember is that this is someone's home. There is typically a list of rules that the host would like you to carry out. They'll want you to take out the trash, bundle up bedsheets, pile up towels, wash your dishes, and clean up after yourself when you leave. As a visitor, you are also rated on Airbnb, so if you want people to invite you to stay in their Airbnb, keep your rating up.

## Hotels

You are most likely already experienced with booking hotels, but here are a few tips to keep in mind:

- Hotels can be much cheaper in some countries. I've stayed in some gorgeous hotels for as low as $20-50 a night. If you are craving beaches but don't want crazy prices, it may be worth your time to fly to South East Asia where the water is warm, hotels are cheap, and the views are beautiful.

- Check for guest satisfaction ratings rather than star ratings. If most of the previous guests loved it, you will likely love it too.

- 1-2-star hotels are generally not as bad as people think they are, depending on the location. If you simply need a basic place to sleep and plan to be out of the room most of the day, these may be the best way to go. Don't forget to check reviews, location, and guest satisfaction ratings to make sure people felt safe, and that the rooms were clean.

- 3-star hotels generally offer shuttle services, free internet, free breakfasts, nice clean rooms, reasonable prices, free parking, and are close to popular destinations.

- 5-Star Hotels - I know some people who travel that only stay in fancy hotels. If you have the money and like the finer things, there are some really cool hotels in this world. Personally, I think they are overrated for the following reasons:

  - You'll be expected to pay for simple things that would be free in other hotels, such as the internet, parking, breakfast, and more

  - Everything on the hotel grounds is overpriced.

  - Most are still basic hotel rooms that offer fancier shampoos.

  - A lot of 5-star hotels offer valet and self-parking. The self-parking tends to be inconvenient and far away from the actual rooms.

## Couchsurfing

www.couchsurfing.com

Couchsurfing is a website with a massive community of travelers. Traditionally, it was simply used as a free place to sleep. Hosts allow travelers to sleep in their homes. It is still a great resource for a free place to stay, but it has since become a way to meet and keep in touch with other travelers as well. It's so massive that you can find Couch Surfers in any major city in the world and in many remote places as well.

I love the website and the community it creates. When used correctly, it is a great way to meet locals, get a free place to sleep, and experience the destination. Each host has their own page where you can see reviews of people they have hosted, people they have stayed with, or people they have hung out with that they met through the website. Some hosts have hundreds of verified reviews.

## Couchsurfing Tips
### For Women:

I no longer recommend Couch surfing as a place to sleep. I only recommend it to meet other people. I've had mostly great experiences sleeping on couches, but the one bad experience was enough to keep me from ever using it again. If you decide to try it anyway, please keep the following things in mind:

- Please be aware that A LOT of men use it as an easy way to meet and sleep with women. If this is not okay with you, it is perfectly acceptable to mention that you are not looking for a hook-up when you request to stay with someone. I write it directly on my profile.

- If all they have to offer is a "shared surface", it means that they plan on sharing a bed. I met a guy who tells me that he's slept with almost every woman that has stayed with him using this method.

- If fighting off the attention of hosts does not appeal to you, research who else has stayed with them. Look for hosts that have hosted people of all genders and ages.

- Reach out to families, women, or couples. You are less likely to be harassed, but not always.

**For Both Women & Men:**

- Know where your money is at all times.

- Read the reviews carefully

- Reach out to the host at least a week in advance, it's harder to get last minute places to sleep.

- Confirm your stay at a day before arrival, it will remind the host that you are arriving and it is a good time to verify directions.

- Make sure you know how to get to the location before the day of arrival.

- Get contact information before the day of arrival.

- Be courteous and have low expectations. Some hosts will have time to party with you and show you around, but many will have busy lives and only offer a place to sleep.

# Chapter 8

## Transportation

*"If you are on a budget, take an Uber to a close bus line, and you can save a ton of money."*

- Steve, USA

My first international flight was into Mexico City, Mexico. My sister was living there, and my mom and I showed up to visit her. We were so excited to see her - it had been months - so when we got to the gate, we were surprised to see that she wasn't there. She didn't have a cell phone back then, and social media was new, so we had no way to reach out to her.

We hung around the airport for a couple of hours waiting for her, but she never showed. Eventually, we realized that she wasn't coming, so we needed to figure out how to get where we were going. Neither of us could speak Spanish other than basic greetings. We tried to find someone who could speak English, but no one could help us. We found a phone system and had been standing there for about 10 minutes trying to figure out how to use it when a man came up and said in English, "Do you need help?"

He let us use his phone card to call our sister and then offered a taxi service to our hotel. We both knew it wasn't the safest route, but at that point, we didn't know what else to do. So we followed him to his "taxi," which was a simple brown car. We were both new to traveling and weren't sure what was normal and what wasn't, so like idiots, WE GOT IN.

Our driver was extremely friendly and chatted away with us the whole way to our hotel. I was sitting on a tire in the backseat and had my luggage sitting on my lap because there was nowhere else to put it. When we arrived at the hotel, we were both so relieved and could not stop laughing.

We took a picture with him, and his car, overpaid him by A LOT and went to our room.

It turns out that my sister thought we were coming the next day. She completely panicked when she got our message. She got all the way to the airport and couldn't find us anywhere. She eventually made her way to the hotel, and we were finally able to meet up. (This story makes me so grateful for modern technology.) When she heard how much we were charged and saw the picture of the car we got in, she had mixed feelings of horror, fear, anger, and laughter.

When it comes to traveling, I don't plan much, but I over-plan when it comes to transportation. Before you leave on any trip, you want to know how you will get from the airport to your lodging, especially in a foreign country.

- If possible, book transportation with your place of lodging

- Make sure you have a plan

- Make sure you have a back-up plan

- Research how much each plan should cost

- Ensure you have access to an ATM in the airport to draw out cash; credit cards are not always an option.

- Pay attention to your landing time, and make sure the transportation method you choose will run at that time.

## Taxis

Taxis are often the safest and fastest ways to get to where you are going. They charge more than most other kinds of transportation but are worth it if you want to be somewhere quickly. I've had some horrible experiences with taxi drivers, so I'm very, very cautious when I get into one. Apparently, I'm not alone. There is an entire website designed to help travelers find reliable transportation without being dependent on taxis at ihatetaxis.com

Here are some tips for riding in taxis:

- Research average prices. Make sure you have an idea of how much a ride will cost before you get in a taxi.

- Pay attention to the meter. I've demanded that a driver stop more than once because I could tell the meter was running higher than it should have been.

- Make a show of mapping your destination on your phone. I don't always have data, so I sometimes pretend. I know this can seem rude, but taxi drivers have been known to take the long way around. One drove my sister around for an hour before dropping her off while she was visiting me in China. He made four times what he should have made. She had no idea until I found out later.

- Be aware that in some countries, you will immediately be bombarded by drivers – and they can be aggressive. If you need one, make sure you have "How much will it cost?" on a translation system, and have them write down the number.

- Research the taxi system in each country before you arrive. Some countries will have reliable taxis; others will have shady taxis. Make sure you are comfortable with the taxi before getting in the cab.

My friend Jon tells this hilarious story of his experience with motor taxis in Cambodia

"I was in Cambodia, teaching English for a year at a school. In Cambodia, they have motorcycle taxis everywhere. They drive around and always kind of slow down and stop in front of you, trying to get you to jump on. One day, I was in a massive rush and trying to go from one school campus to another. I see one of the taxis, so I flag him down and jump on the back and tell him where to go. I knew exactly how much money I would need for the ride, so when we arrived, I tried to give him the money, but he refused to take it! This was really confusing to me because motorcycle taxis are known to overcharge. Until it dawned on me that it WASN'T a motorcycle taxi-it was just some random Cambodian, minding his own business, and I jumped on the back!"

## Rail Transit

If you are looking for options to get from city to city, many countries offer train systems. These systems will even sometimes extend into other countries. The Eurail is a great example of this. They can be pricier than other options but are well worth the extra money when you consider the comfort and ease of riding on a train. I skipped these for the most part in Europe, but found them very affordable in other places such as China

Many cities offer urban rail systems. I love these because, I don't like taking taxis and I prefer to try to get around on my own. Most metros and trains allow passengers to purchase tickets through an automated system, and almost all of them have an English option. If you've never ridden on an urban rail system before, I'd recommend getting a taxi to your hotel before trying to figure out how to use them. It can be overwhelming if you are exhausted from a long flight and have a lot of luggage. If you do decide to take this method, email your lodging and ask them for the route to their location.

Train and Metro Tips:

- Search for train apps for the city you are in and look for an English search option. These apps can help tremendously when you are trying to figure out which lines you need to take.

- Look for a map. Most places of transportation will have a metro map. You'll want to look for your route, look for transitions, and take a picture of it. Notice the first and last stop on the line you are taking. You'll need it later when you are searching for your train.

- Make sure you know which stop you need before arriving at a new place. You don't want to be fumbling around in a train stop trying to figure it out.

- If you go to a booth and say the stop you want to go to, the person will tell you the amount you need to pay and hand you your tickets. You may find this easier than trying to use an automated system.

- If you go to a machine, you may find it a bit confusing at first; some charge by the stop you are going to, some charge by city zones, some charge by the lines you are using, and some only charge a flat fee. Be prepared to stand there a minute as you learn how to purchase tickets.

- When you are on the metro, be mindful of how many stops you've taken and pay attention to the announcements.

As my friend Jon from Switzerland says, *"Look for local train deals. Sometimes, they are much cheaper than express deals. Like from the London airport or the Glacier Express to Switzerland. You can do the exact same thing on local trains for way less money."*

## Boats and Ferries

I've ridden on several ferries and boats throughout my travels. These can be a great way to get from one place to the next, and sometimes more affordable than you might expect. They can also offer a unique way to experience a new place. Cruises, canoeing, kayaking, boat tours, island hopping tours, river cruises are some of the fun ways I've been privileged to enjoy being on the water.

A great example is a popular 5-day boat tour from Panama to Colombia. Tours offer 2-3 days in the San Blas Islands and then cruise on over to Colombia, offering meals, drinks, and many of the things that tourists want to see in the area in one decently priced package.

## Rental Cars and Motorbikes

Both of these options are great ways to see a place. You are able to keep your own schedule and it often allows you to see unique places. Before choosing this route, do your research to find out if it is safe to drive on your own in the country and find out what requirements they have for foreigners to rent. You'll need an International Driver's License in most places, but these are easy to acquire. You can find courses online or classes in your local cities.

It's also important to document the condition of the vehicle BEOFRE you drive it. Take a video, take pictures, or at the very least thoroughly fill out the initial report you are given. In most cases, you won't need it, but it is always possible to be blamed for something that was already a problem before you drove it. If you are wrongly accused, a simple video will be enough proof to avoid paying extra.

## Long Distant Buses

Buses overseas tend to be much nicer than the ones in the United States. If you are on a budget but want to travel around the place you're in, I'd recommend researching buses. Many budget travelers use these and some kind of scoff when I tell them I took a cheap flight or a train. For some, crazy long bus rides are part of their traveling experience. I love the overnight ones because I can sleep through most of the trip.

My friend Nick, from Australia, tells a great story of a long bus trip gone wrong:

This was in the days before the internet on phones, well on my phone at least. I was in Belgrade, Serbia, attempting to rech Sofia, Bulgaria, by bus. Although I couldn't read anything on it as the Serbian alphabet is Cyrillic, I got my ticket and made it onto the bus.

The journey began as usual, but soon we turned off the highway, the number of people on the bus was reducing, the roads were getting windier, and the altitude was increasing. Eventually, there was no one else on the bus, and the driver turned off the engine. We were in a small mountain village. I approached him with my ticket and looked at him in despair. He only spoke Serbian, so we were limited in communication, but it was clear that I'd done something wrong. It started to get dark as he marched off the bus and began a conversation with the only two people in the street. I looked out of the window as they discussed my future. One of the men, a guy around 30, disappeared and came back with a similarly aged friend.

"What are you doing here?" He asked in very clear English. It turned out that he was from the Isle of Man, an island surrounded on all parts by the UK and very much English speaking. He was here in this village of about 300 people with his family visiting his Serbian grandparents. He explained that I'd got on the right bus initially, but I was supposed to change to another bus. Next thing I know, I'm back at their house, and his grandma has served me a plate of Cevapis, with salad, bread, coffee, beer, and limoncello all at once.

After that, my new friend, Richard, suggested we go for a beer. The pub wasn't open, but he knew the publican's son, so he opened it up for us. It was just him, me, his friend who happened to be on the street at the right time, and the publican's son. No one else came in.

I don't recall what we drank, but we had a lot of it, and I'm not sure what time it was when we stumbled back to the house. I was awoken at 4 am. The bus, whose driver had slept in the vehicle overnight, was heading back down the hill. It was the only bus for the day. The whole experience had taken around 12 hours, but it was quite an adventurous 12 hours."

## Local Buses

I recommend them because they are cheap and once you know where you are going and how to pay, they are easy to use. But I admit that I'm kind of terrified of using local buses in foreign countries. I'm not scared for my safety but scared for how quickly I need to move on these things.

The experience goes something like this. You stare at a sign, hoping you can figure out which bus you need when it approaches. It isn't always obvious how to pay or how much it will cost, but you will need to quickly figure it out when it is your turn to pay the driver. Most take change, some take bills, and a few don't take either, because you need a prepaid card. Think of it like a very fast-paced video game. The object is to ride the correct bus, pay the right amount as quickly as you can, listen and pay attention to where you are at all times, and get off at the correct stop. Have fun and good luck!

## Other Forms of Travel Transportation

**Tuk Tuks:** These have different names, depending on where you are in the world. These are REALLY fun to ride because they are like fast golf carts. Some of them are even decked out and play music. The price for these often involves some bargaining; ask other travelers or your hotel how much one should cost.

**BlaBlaCar:** To use this carpooling system, search your route and the day you want to go. Drivers going to the same location on the same day will pop up, and you'll see the driver's reviews and background. They'll generally charge a flat fee, and you'll meet them at a set location and hop in the car. I used this several times in Europe and truly enjoyed each trip.

On a trip from Budapest to Vienna, another passenger lived in Spain. I was planning to visit Spain in a couple of weeks, so she offered to meet up with me and show me around. Just as promised, we met up. She introduced me to a few of her friends, and took me to an adorable Tapas restaurant, where the three of us women shared wine, food, stories, laughter, and even some tears late into the night.

**Uber:** A lot of countries have Uber, and it works just like it does in the United States. Some countries accept only cash, so you'll need to make sure you have some. I like to use Uber because I know the price before I get in the car. Some countries do not have Uber but have similar apps that you can download in English. Ask the guest services helper at your lodging to see what the apps are called, and if foreigners can use it. Please keep in mind that Uber is illegal in some countries. When I was in Colombia, I used it, but it wasn't legal, so I had to get in the front seat and hop out quickly so the "authorities" didn't find out.

Overall Tips for Using Transportation

- Take pictures of maps and directions ahead of time, while you have reliable Wi-Fi.

- Trying something for the first time can seem scary, like buses or metros. You'll feel stupid and rushed at first, but you WILL figure it out. The next time you try, you'll be slightly more confident - and by the end of the next day, you'll have the system down.

- Always remain aware of your location and how to get back to your lodging.

# Chapter 9

## Deciding What to See and Do

*"Don't plan more than 50% of your time. Leave time for navigational errors, random explorations from locals or host's recommendations, and sometimes time to just relax or take a nap. Our trips are so much better when we have lots of flexibility in our schedule. We try to plan one thing per day, and everything else is spontaneous. We make lists of maybes/things we are interested in but will only do them if time allows."*

- Kenisa, USA

The first time I went backpacking across Europe, I had everything perfectly prepared - every train ride, every plane trip, every overnight stay was planned. I printed out maps to every hostel we stayed in and made sure I knew exactly how to get to each of them when we arrived at our destination. This level of planning left no wiggle room for errors or spontaneity. Either would result in not seeing something I'd already paid for and planned. However, it made the trip much easier than it would have been for us as first-time backpackers.

Deciding what to do when you first arrive in a country is the fun part of most people's planning. If you are unsure what to do in a new destination, you can research online. Typically, bloggers and travel websites will have a list of the top things to do and see. If plans thrill you, you can book an entire trip from your living room. If you are not a planner, you may find that these lists are not useful until you arrive somewhere and are not sure of what to do.

## Plan for Leisure Time

One of the best ways to enjoy a trip is to have a day or two in each city with no plans. You can walk around in neighborhoods, go into shops, check out the different foods in grocery stores, try small bakeries or restaurants, find pretty parks to rest or read in or go to a local event.

My friend Melissa describes how she and her husband used their leisure time once while they were in Thailand:

We try to incorporate a couple of leisurely days in our travels. It allows for a little more observation and spontaneity.

On a trip to Thailand, we had scheduled a week in Chiang Mai. While riding around in a tuk-tuk, we kept noticing a poster. Most of it was printed in Thai but included the English phrase: "King's Cup" and showcased the dates that overlapped with our stay. We engaged in the typical miming, pointing, and simplified English to request to be dropped off at this unknown event's location.

Upon arrival, we discovered ourselves watching an international competition of Sepak Takraw. We knew nothing about the sport but learned a lot while watching and had a blast using a travel day to engage in something so unexpected!"

## How Much to Plan

If it is your first time overseas, I recommend planning most of your trip out. Have lodging picked out, know what you want to see and do, and know what to expect with transportation. It will help you decide on future trips - what you think is necessary to plan and not.

At this point in my travels, I don't plan much before arriving somewhere. This is because I'm comfortable with the process of traveling and expecting the unexpected. I typically have an idea of what I want to see, but I wait until I arrive before hashing out details. Almost always, my hostel will have the cheapest ways to see what I want to see. It also leaves room to potentially meet new people and explore with them.

Despite this, there are some things I ALWAYS have planned:

1. The first few nights of lodging.

2. How I will get from the airport to the lodging

3. If I really want to see something, I make sure I don't need to book tickets or a tour ahead of time.

On one of my longer trips, I knew I would do three things: fly in to Japan to visit my friend, meet another friend in India to participate in her wedding ceremony, and spend some time in Vietnam. I bought a one-way ticket into Japan and a one-way ticket out of New Delhi back to Phoenix. The rest of the trip filled itself in as I went. Sometimes, I liked a place and would stay an extra few days, while sometimes, I didn't like it at all and left earlier than I'd planned. Once, I even met a traveler on one part of the trip and a few weeks later, I flew in to see her country to stay with her.

If you have been to a few places and feel ready to keep more of an open schedule, here are a few tips:

1. Ask the people around you for tips. Ask other travelers, hotel clerks, and hostel employees. All of them will tell you what to see and the best way to see it.

2. Ask travelers where they came from and where they are going. If it is something new, you can add it to your list of places to see.

3. Try planning one or two places around a cool hostel or hotel. In Gili Air, Indonesia, I stayed at a hostel called Captain Coconuts. It was beautiful. There were cute private huts, but I chose to stay in the dorms. The room I slept in was in a hut with open windows and beds that hung from the ceiling. I loved it so much that I stayed a couple of extra days. Such a fun way to sleep!

4. Be open to changing course, especially if you meet others to travel with. When I traveled to Croatia, I'd planned on visiting Split and Dubrovnik. However, what I did not plan was meeting two hilarious Israelis and their funny friends. Instead of seeing Dubrovnik alone, I spent the next few days exploring waterfalls in Croatia in a car filled with great people.

5. You can plan out one or two days and keep the rest open.

6. Read travel blogs.

7. Be open to going to a lesser-known place instead of a famous one. I've seen some stunning places that most people have never heard of because someone told me that a particular site was better than the famous one.

## Travel Fatigue

Depending on how long your trip is, it is entirely possible to get "sick of" seeing the same things all the time. If you've spent days, or even weeks, seeing temples and shrines, it's easy to get a little disenchanted with the idea of seeing the next one. I have a good guy friend of mine, who is an avid traveler, who always says, "Make sure to take a vacation from your vacation." Meaning, find a way to take a break. If you are in cities, get out in nature. If you are in nature, take a break in a city. In other words, do something different than what you are doing.

## Vacation Tours

Tours can sometimes be the easiest way for someone to travel. If you are reading this book and all the details are overwhelming rather than exciting, I'd recommend trying to book a tour or a travel agent. The trips will generally cost more than a simple budget trip, but you'll have every part of your trip taken care of for you.

Tours often include everything, including flights, transportation, hotels, tourist attractions, and even some meals. Some tours offer multiple locations, so you can see more than one place. There are some great deals on websites such as *Travelzoo.com.* Keep in mind that if a tour is super cheap, there will likely be some bumps along the way. Your hotel might not be as nice as you hoped for, you may end up waiting longer than you expected at times, or a section of the tour may not be included. Still, this is a great option for those who want an easy way to see other places.

## Travel Agents

Travel Agents, the legitimate ones, are very educated on how to help you plan the perfect vacation around your budget. If you long to see Bora Bora, they will help book a place, flight, and excursions. If you think Bora Bora is too much money, they know other places with a similar experience that you can visit instead. Good travel agents have taken classes and are also experienced travelers, so they can use both book knowledge AND personal experiences to help you find the perfect vacation.

# Preparing for the Trip

# Chapter 10

## Packing

*"You don't need as many things as you think you do. I've lived for literally years with only one small backpack, and it felt like the ultimate freedom. Sure, you get bored wearing the same clothes a lot, but you can always swap it out at a charity shop, etc., and it's so worth it when you don't have to lug a heavy suitcase from point A-B every time you go somewhere new. It also makes flights super cheap if you can get away with just hand luggage in Europe."*

- Elinor, UK/Denmark

I was in Santorini, Greece, with my friend. We were supposed to meet a taxi driver outside our hostel at 4:30am. We set an alarm for 4 am and fell asleep. Seemingly minutes later, I woke back up and something felt…off. I opened my eyes, looked at the clock, and it was 4:23 am.

4:23am?!! AAAAAGGGHHH!! All hell broke loose. My friend had a rude awakening, and likely the neighbors, because I was screaming "WE HAVE 7 MINUTES!!!" A flurry of activity happened after that. I was half awake, laughing, and was shoving everything I could find into a badly packed, overfilled bag as fast as I could. I looked over at my friend, and she wasn't doing any better. She was trying her hardest to shove her pretty new sunhat into her bag yelling, "WHY DID I BUY THIS STUPID HAT?!" We left our room 5 minutes late, ran outside in a panic, only to find….nothing. The driver ended up being 20 minutes late.

This story is exactly why you want to have a good bag, a good packing routine and the right amount of stuff.

## What kind of bag should I bring?

A good travel bag is essential. You want something easy to maneuver, comfortable to pick up, and sturdy. A good bag allows you to get into it easily. You should be able to put things back in the same spot every time and pack or unpack within 5 minutes. If you need to find your toothbrush, it should take less than ten seconds to locate it.

I've seen all kinds of bags while traveling, and like a lot of travelers, I've tried many of them. These days, I have such an efficient packing system that I can't help but feel sorry for those who seem to be behind me in bag/packing knowledge. When people tell me they need 30+minutes to pack up, when people enter a hostel room looking exhausted from carrying a huge bag, or when people have all of their stuff sprawled out everywhere because they are trying to get organized, I always want to share what I've learned.

## What is a Day Pack?

Almost all travelers that I've run into have two bags: a daypack and a travel bag. A day pack is a small bag that travelers use while touring their destination. It comes in handy for multiple things such as day trips, hiking, or carrying larger items like a book or water bottles. The idea is to keep this pack light and only use it for touring. All the big stuff goes into the travel bag.

## What bags do you recommend for traveling?

These are the kinds of bags that I recommend. There are specific suggestions, for point of reference, but you might be able to find cheaper, secondhand versions at thrift stores or on the internet.

- **Carry-On Travel Bag that opens like a suitcase:** Like the Osprey Porter 46 Pack. Make sure it has supportive straps. I had one that didn't offer the support I needed, and I ended up in a German hospital with terrible back pain.

- **Spinner Roller Carry-On Bag:** Like the eBags Mother Lode 22 Inches Carry-On Spinner. Not as cool, but practical. This is what I currently use. It turns out there is a lot less cobblestone than the travel world would have you believe. Not to mention that most of the newer kinds can roll over almost anything. I prefer to pick up a bag for a couple of minutes if I need to, rather than carrying it on my back for an entire trip.

- **Carry-On Sized Roller that converts into a backpack:** Like the Osprey 42L Wheeled Carry-on Travel Bag. I loved this bag. The only reason I don't still use it is that the straps took up so much room, and I only used them once. I realized it was easier to just pick up the bag for tricky parts, and the straps became a waste of space.

## A Huge Backpacker's Backpack

Don't do it!!! This is like the advice your wise old grandma gives you. She knows you'll probably ignore it, but she can't help but share the good advice anyway. I started my travels with a backpacker's backpack. I looked so cool with that thing on my back. I knew I was legit; the mirror and the camera told me so. Never mind the fact that I was out of shape, had no upper body strength whatsoever, and my packing ability wasn't the best, I HAD to have it.

Here are the two main reasons that I don't recommend them:

- Weight: Even with the support straps, it's uncomfortable to wear after a certain length of time. If you're planning on walking around, it starts to get heavy. You'll find yourself shifting, setting it down, and trying to ignore the weight on your back. The worst is you may find yourself avoiding sights and places because you'll need to carry your backpack to get to them.

- Packing: A backpacker's backpack will make this almost impossible to locate things quickly and easily. You have two choices, you either dump out the entire content or root around desperately hoping to find what you're looking for - and half the time, you end up dumping it anyway. Even with packing cubes (God's gift to travelers, by the way), these things are a pain to pack and unpack.

If you're a beginner and dreaming of getting those famous backpack shots while wandering Europe, I wouldn't blame you if you decided to do it anyway. Just make sure:

1. The backpack fits you. Make sure the straps are in the correct places, and that weight of your bag is something that you can comfortably carry for at least an hour.

2. Use Packing Cubes!

3. Work out. You'll need the muscles. Take it from a pro - you don't want to injure your back.

## Questions to ask yourself before buying a bag:

1. Does this bag have a high rating?

2. Do the zippers work well when full? (Put a blanket or something in it to test it out.)

3. Do the wheels turn and maneuver easily?

4. Is it something I can pick up and carry for a while if necessary?

## How much to pack?

You'll notice I say "Carry-On" a lot. There is a reason for that. I'd already been to several countries when I decided to switch to a carry-on. I remember the effort it took to narrow down what I'd need for several different climates – Four and a half months of travel. It seemed impossible at first. I'd read somewhere to get it down to the essentials and then divide it in half.

I remember staring at each item, trying to figure out what to get rid of. Then I did, one by one – with no regrets. It was SO much easier to get around. No more avoiding locations because I didn't want to roll or carry a huge bag. No more relentlessly digging trying to find something. No more running over people's toes with my giant bags in small or crowded spaces (like trains or buses.)

Here are a few tips to help you pack for a carry-on:

- Use packing cubes - they will help you organize and sort your stuff.

- Search for "Capsule Closets" or "Capsule Travel Wardrobe" on the internet.

- Plan to use layers to help you with the weather rather than bulky coats.

- Bring a lot of underwear. I bring two weeks worth for my longer trips and one for every day for my shorter ones. You can get away with wearing the same shirt and pants several times, but underwear? Ewww. Washers and dryers are a precious commodity while traveling and are not always convenient or available. I met a guy that told me he just buys new underwear on his trips, so he wouldn't have to worry about doing laundry so much.

- Roll your clothes, rather than folding them. It helps eliminate some of the wrinkles, and it saves space.

- Try to put everything back in the same place every time.

- Don't overpack your bag. I know it's tempting to fill the space with last-minute "I HAVE to bring this!" things. You'll find stuff along the way that you'll want to take with you.

## Preparing for the Plane

You know that feeling you have when you are so busy you can hardly think? You say to yourself, "I'll read that book when I have time." Or "I'll watch that movie when I have time." Or "I will think about this later." Do you want to know one of the best times to get these done? In transit.

When people think of flying, they think of being crammed into economy class (unless you are one of the lucky ones), eating mediocre food, getting cramps, and counting down the minutes until they can get off of the plane. I'm not sure there is anyone who doesn't feel a sense of relief when it's their turn to get out of the seat and walk off the plane. However, the time during transit is an excellent chance to catch up on reading, music, thoughts, conversation, writing, work, or even sleep. You have nothing to do but just be. You'll enjoy the ride a lot more if you are relaxing and taking advantage of the downtime.

What should I bring on the plane?

- Earplugs

- Eye Mask

- Heaviest of your clothing - jeans, coat, sweatshirts. Planes are often cold, plus you can use them for pillows, lumbar support, or blankets.

- Socks

- Your favorite snacks

- Toothbrush/toothpaste for long flights

- Travel pillow

- Charger

- Earbuds

- Movie, book, or charged phone

During my first backpacking trip to Europe, my friend and I were in our mid-twenties and wanted to be legit, so we tried to "rough it" the best we could by not bringing any hair products and minimal makeup. It turned out to be a horrible idea and a "mistake" neither of us has since repeated. We have pictures of us in the most beautiful, iconic places, looking, well… awful.

One of our favorite stories, in light of all this, was meeting two gorgeous girls in Santorini that we dubbed "The younger, prettier versions of ourselves." They were so much fun, and we had the most wonderful day with them. After spending an entire day swimming around in Santorini's beaches, we all split up and agreed to meet up for dinner.

My friend and I decided to shop during this time. When we met up an hour later, we noticed our new friends looking fresh and lovely, while my friend and I looked like drowned rats. (sunburned, drowned rats.)

While at the restaurant, it didn't take long before some guys noticed our friends. The guys made their way over to the table and started aggressively hitting on them. These girls were smart and handled them like champs. One of the guys noticed a hotel key, and obnoxiously picked it up and asked if this is where the girls were staying (It was). I grabbed it out of his hand and pretended it was mine. I said dryly, "That's mine. You're going to be sorely disappointed."

The guy dropped the key when he realized it was mine and ignored me, but my self-deprecating comment had my friend and I cracking up. We still laugh about it to this day.

# Chapter 11

## Leaving the Country

*"Always have just enough cash, but not too much because of those sneaky pick-pocketers you always read about. It's a delicate balance. Little bars in little towns out in the middle of nowhere don't always have credit card machines and trying to find some way to pull cash when the rest of the town is asleep is not fun."*

- Kenisa, USA

## Money

It's important to know how you will access cash before you get to the country you visit. There are a few exchange options, but I highly recommend using an ATM if you prefer the easier route. According to most travelers, it's almost always a better financial option, and it is far less stressful.

You WILL need cash. In some places, you may be able to use a credit card, but you'll find that many countries still depend on cash for shops, restaurants, and transportation. You will most likely need it to get from the airport to your lodging.

Accessing an ATM is the first thing I do when I fly into an airport. I take out enough money to cover my hotel, transportation, and food for the next couple of days. For me, it comes to about $45 a day, so I use my phone to quickly calculate the exchange rate and pull out the amount I need according to that.

If you plan on spending $100 a day, search what $100USD is in the currency of the country you are visiting, and it will give you the amount. Round it up and multiply it by the number of days you want to cover.

If you do decide to go the money exchange route, try to avoid exchanging money at the airport. The fees are much higher. If you can, try to exchange it in your home country rather than the country you are visiting.

## Credit Cards

Try to get a credit card that has no international fees. You'll still be charged a fee from the place you are visiting, but the credit card you chose won't charge you any more on top of it.

Before you leave the country, call your bank and your credit card companies to let them know where you will be visiting. To prevent theft, banks and card companies will shut down any suspicious activity and render your card useless until you call them. I once had this happen just as I had arrived at 10:30 pm in Indonesia. I had no way of phoning them because the Wi-Fi wasn't working and taxi cabs only took cash. I ended up asking the hotel to front me the money. It was pretty stressful!

## Passport

Don't let anyone tell you that you won't need your passport. There are a few exceptions if you are on a cruise or close to a border town, but you do not want to find out the hard way that you actually need your passport. I've heard of people stopping in a country and having a tough time getting out, even though others in the same group got by just fine. Bring your passport everywhere with you.

**If you have a passport, make sure that your expiration date is more than six months prior to your departure date.** For example, if your trip is in May, make sure it doesn't expire before December. Many countries will not let you in if your passport expires in less than six months.

You also need to make sure you have enough blank pages. Some countries require an entire page!

If you don't have a passport yet, do yourself a favor and get it right away - even if you haven't booked your flights yet. Here are the steps you will need to take to get a passport.

1. Go to
   *https://travel.state.gov/content/travel/en/passports/how-apply.html*

2. Fill out a form called (DS-11)

3. Prepare payment for the application fee.

4. Get passport photos. Local Pharmacies are a great way to get these done quickly. They are strict about these, so just have them done. Always get extras and save them in case you need them for visas.

5. Go to a passport center. Passport applications cannot be submitted online. Bring the following items with you:
   a. Original Proof of Citizenship (Like a birth certificate)
   b. Passport Photo
   c. Photo ID Document (driver's license)
   d. A photocopy of the front and back of the citizenship document and photo ID document
   e. Payment

## Visa

Depending on both where you are going and where you are coming from, you may need a visa to enter your destination country. Some countries have a fairly easy visa process, and you can submit it online; but with others, you'll need to submit paperwork and pictures months ahead. I've heard of people flying into other countries, not realizing that they needed a visa, and they get stuck at the airport or are sent back home. It's important to know exactly what the country wants from you when you enter their country.

- Each country will have an official website that will tell you what visa requirements to expect.

- Some countries will have visa service websites, making the process easier. It is typically more expensive than going directly. Watch out for scams.

- Some countries will require an entry fee. Most range from $20-200. Most will allow you to pay with a card or in dollars, but some will require it to be paid in local cash.

## Theft Preparation

We all hope it won't happen, but unfortunately, sometimes it does. I've been lucky to have gone unscathed so far, but theft has occurred to many of my traveling friends. Wallets are the most common, but some have lost purses, jewelry, bags, and a few have lost all of their luggage.

Those who come prepared are bummed but have a plan to move forward in case it happens. I will cover more about being safe and preventing theft but here are some quick planning tips in case it happens.

- Print out two or three copies of your passport, flight plans, and IDs. Put each copy in a different place: in your bags, purse, or luggage. Hide them if possible.

- Hide one of your credit cards in a different bag. If your bag has a hidden zipper, put it there. If not, I would suggest cutting a discreet hole. I have a friend that does this, and it paid off when he got his wallet stolen. He was frustrated but was able to use his hidden credit card for the rest of the trip.

- Write down or take a picture of the telephone numbers on the back of each of your credit cards and of your passport. If they are stolen, it will help to have the number readily available.

## Data or SIM Cards

If your phone plan doesn't involve international calls and data, and you think you'll want to use the internet on your phone a lot, you may want to consider buying a SIM card. I have done this multiple times, especially when I was to be in the country for a while. It's not necessary, Wi-Fi is everywhere, and sometimes, it's nice to be unplugged while you are sightseeing, but I understand wanting to have quick access to information.

In most places, it will be much cheaper to pay for a SIM card when you arrive. Our plans in the U.S. are pretty high in comparison to most areas, with a few exceptions. For example, when I was in Vietnam, I only paid about $8 for a month's worth of data. I just walked right into a cell phone store with "I need a SIM card" on my translate app.

If you decide to purchase a SIM card, make sure you don't lose your old one! They are tiny and easy to lose.

## VPN

A VPN is a Virtual Private Network. These come in handy if the country you are visiting blocks certain websites. I lived in China for 6 months, and I needed a VPN to access Facebook, Google, and my email. I've also needed it a few times in other countries when my work websites were being blocked.

A VPN service blocks your real IP, deterring website services from determining your location. You choose a VPN from a particular country, and your IP address appears to be in that place. There are many reasons someone might try to use a VPN, but for a traveler, it helps them access websites that might otherwise be blocked.

There are many companies out there that offer VPNs. If you are going to a location that might block websites, research one ahead of time and choose the one you think will work for you. Make sure it is month-to-month, allowing you to cancel when you want.

## Vaccinations, Medicine, and Prescriptions

Before leaving for any trip, it is wise to research what vaccines you may need for the country or region you visit. I only get vaccines if required, but I know many people feel safer if they follow recommendations.

Please visit *www.nc.cdc.gov/travel* to find out what vaccines you may need.

If you take any prescribed medicine, fill up before you go on your trip. I also recommend researching pharmacies in other countries. You may find your prescription much cheaper there. When I was young, my mom, who is a nurse, went to Mexico to stock up on antibiotics and some other basic things that would be much more expensive here. Unfortunately, I told my teacher that my mom was in Mexico buying drugs, which led to many questions for my poor mother.

I always bring Claritin and Ibuprofen with me when I travel. Ibuprofen can usually be found locally, but I like to have a supply ready.

While I was in the San Blas Islands, my roommate and I made the same mistake of brushing our teeth with the water. Both of us should have known better, but out of habit, we accidentally did it. I've gotten traveler's sickness multiple times, and every time, I wished I brought something for it. Local places have medications, but accessing them isn't always easy, especially if there is a language barrier.

## Custom and Entry Forms

Each country has entry forms and custom sheets that are required to be filled out before entry. Most airlines will provide these for you in the last hour before landing. If you do not receive one, flag down a flight attendant to ask for one. It's much easier to fill it out on the plane. The forms are also available at the airport, and you can fill them out before getting in line. You will need the address of your first destination, your flight number, and some countries require return flight information as well. If you like to be prepared, you can print these out before leaving your country and have them ready. Consider checking out which items are okay to bring, which items you need to claim, and which items are not allowed.

If the country requires a special visa, they might need a specific form be filled out as well. You'll want to print this before leaving your country.

**Here are some things that you may want to consider:**

- Register your trip with your embassy: This is a free service that will allow you to receive the latest security information about the country you are visiting.

- Purchase Insurance: Travel insurance plans will help cover any medical emergencies, trip cancellations, trip interruptions, medical evacuations, and lost, damaged, or stolen luggage. Just beware of the fine print; sometimes, they are only covered under certain circumstances, and you'll want to know upfront, before discovering that your claim doesn't get covered.

## Useful Travel Apps

- Google Translate: You can download an offline version to use when you don't have Wi-Fi access. This has helped me many times!

- WAZE: A map app

- Maps.me: a map app that you can download and use offline, very useful in stressful "I'm lost" situations.

- Couchsurfing: A community of travelers

- Travel Zoo: Great travel deals

- Uber: Transportation app that can save you money while traveling, if the country allows it

- Rome2Rio: Tells you the different ways to get from here to there. It will search for flights, train routes, buses, and more. It usually includes links, and you can easily book tickets.

- Google Voice: Allows you to call home if necessary

- Skype: Video app

- WhatsApp: A texting app that many countries use to keep in contact with each other.

# Being Present

# Chapter 12

## Safety

*"Do some research on the country's laws. Some laws are very STRICT."*

- Augusto from Peru

My friend Geno tells a story of getting a ride from a stranger in Brazil:

> When I was in Brazil, I got off a bus in a small town with my roller bag. A woman in front of me kept staring at me, then crossed to street to be on the other side.
>
> After a bit, she yelled in Portuguese somewhat aggressively, "Where are you going?!" I answered, and she replied, "Where are you from?" I told her I was from the USA and she suddenly got super friendly and asked where I was going and what I was looking for.
>
> She had never heard of the hotel I was staying at, so she told me to wait for her husband to pull up. Her husband pulled up with two kids and offered to give me a ride to look for the hotel. After driving around, we finally found the hotel.
>
> As they were dropping me off, the woman got motherly and told me, "NEVER EVER get in a car with strangers in Brazil. Please be more careful! It's okay because you're with me, but please be safe." Then she gave me a huge hug and left me at my hotel.

One of the biggest concerns that people have with traveling is safety. Before I go into things you want to be cautious of, I want you to understand that these are just precautions to take when you travel, as long as you are mindful of your surroundings, know where your stuff is at all times, and don't follow people to unknown places, you'll likely be fine.

One of the best parts of my trips is meeting new people and experiencing unexpected adventures. Some of those adventures have been in situations that have not always been the safest option, and grandma would most certainly not approve. I am one of the more cautious travelers that I've run into, but I have taken chances just like any other traveler. Rely on your instincts and use your best judgment.

Before you continue reading about precautions, please keep these two things in mind:

1. This section could scare you from ever wanting to venture out. Try to keep in mind that these are meant to help guide you into a safe trip, not scare you away from travel.

2. You could run into any of the issues below IN YOUR HOME COUNTRY. You are never completely safe.

"Don't go there; it's dangerous." One of the more amusing things that happens is that people from my country tend to perceive our country as safer than most of the world. Depending on where you are in my country, that may be somewhat true, but our cities are not known to be safe at all. In fact, many people avoid coming to the United States because of how dangerous they perceive it to be. Some of it comes from exaggerated accounts of gun violence from the media and movies, but some of it is quite true. When you look at our crime rates, they are often much higher than other places; even other countries infamous for being "unsafe."

While talking with co-workers at work in China, one of them brought up the fact that they would never come to the USA because of how dangerous it was. They were worried about getting shot. I told them that it wasn't that scary, and that I felt safe at home - until I looked at my phone and read that people were getting shot on the freeway. Some lunatic was standing on bridges and shooting cars, a humbling moment for sure. That would never happen in China. Other crazy things happen, but not mass shootings.

Although there are some places that I choose not to go to for safety reasons, there are many countries that I've visited that made my relatives nervous because of their reputation - in spite of the fact I was statistically safer in those places.

If you are worried about being in danger in a place you want to visit, compare the crime rates there to a major city that you'd feel comfortable visiting in the USA. If you feel comfortable visiting New York or LA, for instance, you'll likely find yourself feeling safe in many other countries.

Go to your government website for travel advisories for each country you plan to visit.

## Tips for Remaining Safe

## 1. Try Not to Look Lost

If you are in a country known for pickpocketing and basic scams, try to keep maps, guidebooks, and confused faces inside cafés and hotels. Nothing stands out to a scammer more than a lost tourist. Just duck into a coffee shop o hotel if you are in a hurry. If you need help, ask an employee in a shop or hotel. If a local approaches you and asks if you need assistance, take them up on it, but be mindful of your stuff and pay attention to where you are, especially if you are being led somewhere.

## 2. Be Cautious of Locals

People hate this advice. If the idea of traveling is to mingle and get to know local culture, how can I advise people to be cautious? Hear me out. If you are on the street and a local approaches you, there is a good chance that he or she wants something from you, most likely money, and he or she will simply try to sell you something. Just keep it mind that it could be more sinister, so always be mindful of your stuff and don't go anywhere with a local if you are alone.

In places that don't see many tourists, it's likely that the local just wants to be friendly and is interested in you as a person. However, if you are in a tourist-heavy location, a local has seen a thousand people who look like you, with your same story, and is generally not as interested in foreigners. Keep your guard up in these kinds of places.

If you do want to meet locals, there are better ways. Please read the chapter on "How to Meet People" for more ideas on meeting locals. It's generally safer than trusting someone who approaches you.

## 3. Dangers of Partying

"You need to lighten up," a guy said to me one night. I had stopped to have a beer with him and about ten other people, and it was apparent the guy was hoping to sleep with me. Unfortunately for that guy, I had a tour at 7:30 in the morning, and it was already 11:30 pm. I told him, "I'll be pretty damn light in the morning when I'm not hungover on a boat, and I've had a decent night's sleep."

There are times I drank too much and stayed out too late, but these days, I find myself much more grateful that I chose not to have that last drink or stay out for those last few hours. What is it that I'm missing? Someone throws up. Someone cries. Someone starts grinding on every available human around them. It is all the same; no matter what country I'm in, those last few hours are rarely ever worth my time.

I recognize that for a lot of younger travelers, partying is part of the reason they travel. Drinking in a foreign country feels different, and they want to experience the party life everywhere. As long as people are making smart decisions, I say *do what you gotta do*. However, the stupidest and most unsafe stories I've heard in the travel world almost always involve partying. Whether you are drinking, trying drugs, or going home to sleep with a stranger, TRY to be as vigilant as possible.

- Make sure you are with people that you trust well enough to take care of you if you drink too much.

- I've heard of people waking up in the streets, alone, covered in their own vomit.

- Always keep an eye on your drink - even if you are a man!!

- If you plan to go home with someone, always mention to whoever it is that you need to take a picture of the person and the address of where you are going and send it to a friend. If someone makes you feel bad about this, it's on them. I've heard stories too awful to share, and it's worth slightly offending someone to have this safety measure in place.

- It is YOUR responsibility to know the laws when you are traveling – extremely important! There are countries where you could spend your life in jail for doing drugs. There are countries where you could get flogged, beaten, or even killed for not obeying the laws. Travelers do not get special rights. DO NOT break the law in order to party. It's stupid and dangerous. Again, make sure you know what the laws are before partaking in anything.

## 4. Advice for Women

Unfortunately for us women, we have to be extra careful when we travel. We want to be independent and we deserve to be treated as equals, but in many places around the world, the men have NOT gotten the memo. Consider bringing something like a safety whistle in case something comes up.

If you are passing a group of men, try not to make eye contact. This is especially difficult if you come from a culture that acknowledges people passing by with a nod, or a smile. Try to refrain from this habit. Look straight ahead and ignore any comments or looks if you do not want to talk to the person approaching you. Ignore that ingrained urge to be polite if you don't want to be. Remember that you don't owe anyone a conversation.

My friend Lisa tells a story of a time she was in Thailand with some friends. They met a guy who'd been in Bangkok for a while, and he offered to show her around. He ended up taking her to a strip bar, which made her feel pretty uncomfortable. As the night went on, they moved to different areas of the club, and what she saw got riskier. He drank a ton of beer and didn't seem to be aware that she wasn't drinking much. Eventually, he made a move on her, and even though she said no, he wouldn't stop pressuring her to sleep with him. She ultimately lied and told him she was on her period. After that, he left her alone, but she saw him the next day with his arms around another female tourist.

"He never tried to justify or explain the location, and I can't justify or explain why I stayed. It's not an experience I would necessarily recommend. If it is something that interests you, fine. If it's something that appalls you, it's worth avoiding as there are plenty of other wonderful things about visiting Bangkok, and in that situation, you feel very powerless to do anything that will make it seem right.

So, I share that story to shed a tiny bit of light on that side of Bangkok life.. And to also add my voice to the many that, while traveling or not, no one should ever have to keep saying no or coming up with excuses to try to get out of doing something they don't want to do, especially sex."

## 5. Advice for Men

You have some dangers too, depending on where you are in the world. A common thing happens is when a group of pretty locals approach guys on the street. They will have some drinks, take them to a predetermined place, and steal everything they have on them. I've even heard of men being enticed into "special massage" parlors and being forced to pay their full credit limit. Although it can happen to women, men are more likely to be lured into a drunken brawl. If some local guy is egging you on and threatening you, keep your head low and try to get out of there. There is no telling what he or his friends are capable of doing, and your pride is not worth ending up in jail or severely injured.

## 6. Know Local Clothing Regulations

If you are going to a place that is not as economically advanced as where you are from, do not bring expensive clothes and bags. Wear casual clothing. I promise you can still look good in pictures in outfits that don't scream to the world, "I'm rich!" If you are a fashion lover, research travel capsule closet ideas for ways to look good without compromising your money or safety.

You especially need to think about what you will wear in terms of modesty. In some places, it is as simple as entering a different culture and offending locals by not adhering to their modesty standards. In other locations, you could be sexually assaulted, followed, or even thrown in jail. I've been to a few places where my white face meant "easy." No matter how modestly I dressed, I was followed, called out to, and even groped a few times.

Shorts, for example, are not worn in many cultures. I arrived in Penang, Malaysia after 2 hours of sleep on an overnight flight. I immediately met some travelers who asked if I wanted to tour the city with them. It was really hot and humid, so I threw on a tank top and shorts and took off with them without thinking. It didn't take long for me to discover that I was immodestly dressed. I wasn't over the top, and there were other foreign women dressed similarly, but the stares I received made me pretty self-conscious. From then on, I made sure I was covered more while in that city.

In most places you will visit, your regular clothing will be fine unless you are going into places of religious worship. Most sites will expect you to have your shoulders and knees covered. It's always a good idea to carry a wrap with you if you plan to go into religious establishments.

## 7. Advice for USA Citizens

If you are from the United States, you should probably be aware that even our homeless people are considered rich, compared to much of the world. The world sees us as people with a lot of money, so when you go into their restaurants, shops, and hotels, they will treat you as a source of great wealth. For this reason, I do not advise that you proudly announce you are from the United States. Let that information be vague unless you are specifically asked.

As a US citizen, another thing to be aware of is - prepare yourself for this – some people don't like us. To them, we are just loud, arrogant, attention-seeking, and rude. For others though, they absolutely hate us. Our powerful leaders have made decisions that have left their families desolate, homeless, jobless, or worse, dead. Without getting into politics and the reasons why these things have happened, or whether you even believe it to be true, just please be aware that proudly announcing that you are "American" isn't always the wisest course of action. I've been to places that I've lied and told people I was from a different country. Part of it for my safety, and part of it was to avoid the haunted and sad look that crossed their faces when I said, "America."

If you are not from the USA, do a bit of research to ensure that it is safe or wise to tell someone where you are from in the place you are visiting.

## 8. Research Race-Based Experiences

My advice in this area is limited because I'm white, and I can't speak for the experiences of others traveling. But I can tell you that racism is rampant all over the world and to be careful. If you are of another race, I will not attempt to tell you where you are safe and what experiences you will have. PLEASE research the country you are traveling to.

I've met people from all over the world and of all different races traveling, so your options are not limited. However, just like in your home country, you need to be aware of where it is safe for you to travel and where it isn't. I would advise finding travel bloggers of your ethnic background to see which places they have felt the most welcome.

If you are white, you will often be treated nicely, but you will be seen as a rich person in many places, and a target for theft. We are often treated well, but there are exceptions. I've been followed in stores, kicked out of cabs and restaurants, had clerks terrified to talk to me, had stores refuse to help me, been stopped by police in public places and asked for proof of residency, had locals scared to sit next to me, even had people think I was a terrorist (Russian), and more. I'm grateful that these experiences have been limited, but these things do happen. Just use these experiences to be more aware of how others must feel in similar situations and be grateful that these experiences are exceptions rather than rules to your life.

If you are a white woman, it's good to be aware that white women are used in porn, condom commercials, and are thought of as easy in some parts of the world. I once had a traveler tell me that a guy came up to her, groped her, and pulled out money to buy her. She had to shove him several times before he finally left her alone. This is an extreme case, but you will see evidence of this kind of thinking in the way local men look at you, speak to you, and treat you. Be aware of the country's reputation before visiting. In many places, you'll be safe, and it will just be more of an annoyance.

## 9. Choose Your Bags Wisely

Purses and luggage: Don't travel with flashy name-brand bags unless you are going somewhere that is known to be safe or if you are already familiar with the area. If you are carrying an expensive bag AND looking at a map, you will be a prime target for theft.

When I travel, I keep the most important items near me at all times. Cash, most credit cards, my phone, my passport, and my Vaseline (what? I've got dry lips.) It all goes into a bland looking, small purse that is long enough to go over my shoulder and across my body. I also tend to grip it as I'm walking, especially if I'm somewhere known for pickpocketing. If it is a cold place, I'll wear my bag under my jacket. If I'm at a restaurant, I often loop my arm through the strap before hanging it or place it on my lap. There are times when I've even slept with it. Some people have blankies; I had my precious purse. It may seem extreme, but I have NEVER had anything stolen. I also prefer to grip a purse than to wear a money belt.

Money belts are belts that are strapped to your body under your clothing. You can store money, cards, and even a passport. It is convenient for those who want the most security. I'd especially recommend it to men because they don't tend to have a place to store their valuables. Backpacks are great, but they are easier to access than a tiny purse strung across the front of your body. If you are a man and prefer to carry your wallet, put it in the front pocket. You are far less likely to have someone rummaging around up there than in the back.

Tips for Bags:

- The smaller, the better. Smaller bags are easier to keep track of.

- If you are in a crowded place, be it the subway, a street, or a tourist attraction, turn your day pack, so you are wearing it in the front rather than the back.

- If you don't have a day pack yet, consider a small bag specifically made for traveling. They are often made with anti-theft features such as hidden zippers.

- NEVER take your eyes off of your luggage or bags when you are in transition. You need to know where they are at all times.

- Some travelers bring tiny locks for backpacks and luggage zippers. It keeps people from rummaging through it.

- Don't store anything of great value in a checked bag. Things do get stolen out of them while in baggage handling.

## 10. Money Rules

Do not pull out large amounts of cash in public. Try your hardest to be discreet when you are counting money to hand over. Count bills carefully and lay them out so you can present them to the person, where they can see the bills too. (keeps them from trying to claim you only gave them a 5 when you actually gave a 50.)

Use local currency. Many countries will allow you to use US dollars, but the conversion rate is really high, and you'd get whatever you want to buy much cheaper in local cash.

I always check ATMs for credit card skimmers and hidden cameras. If the card scanner is loose, if there appears to be a small attachment on the card reader, or the card is not going in smoothly, I wait. If the keyboard is spongy, I wait. If there is no way to completely cover the keypad, I wait. This is overly cautious, but it makes me feel safe.

## 11. Being Nice

At the end of a couple of months of traveling solo, I met up with some friends. At first, they were a bit taken aback by how cold and rude I was to people approaching me. I didn't even realize the necessary armor I was putting up. A man walked up to our group and tried to sell us a carriage, and I stepped in front of everyone and said, "No." and walked off only to turn around and see my friends still talking to him. I'd spent months with people like him approaching me, so I was pretty comfortable saying no. It wasn't personal for either of us, and I've learned it was necessary for me to be blunt. It took them forever to shake the guy, whereas he knew right away it not to bother with me.

When I travel, I try to be ready for anything. I'm cautious, continually scanning the area around me, hanging on to my boring purse, and I'm wary when someone approaches. If someone is trying to sell me something, I no longer feel bad saying no or ignoring them. I've had too many rude salespeople shove their items in my face while I'm trying to walk. If someone is trying to talk to me, I no longer feel bad, politely saying, "I'd like to be alone, but have a nice day." and walking off. I've had too many men try to guilt-trip me into spending time with them.

Since I'm often a woman traveling alone, I'm very careful about who I give my time, money, and friendliness to, these things are reserved for other travelers or people I have a good sense of. It has served me well; my judgment and demeanor have kept me safe.

## 12. Be Aware of the Mountain of Scams

There are tons of scams out there. Whenever I hear a new story, it always freaks me out before arriving in a new country. While I never let it stop me, I do make sure I'm being vigilant while out and about. There are too many scams to mention, but here are some popular ones:

- A person of authority comes up to you and demands that you pay a fine or asks to see your luggage or bag and then steals it.

- An unauthorized person tries to sell you fake tickets.

- People selling knock-offs lead you back into a dark alley and won't let you go until you purchase something.

- Locals quickly switch out a smaller bill for a larger one and claim you gave them the wrong amount.

- One person distracts you while the other grabs your belongings.

- Locals offer to take you to a local spot, then stick you with a bill.

Almost every well-traveled person I've met has been scammed in one way or another. If it happens to you, try your best to shake it off and move on. Don't let the jerk who scammed you ruin your trip.

I was in Doha, Qatar, one of the safest cities in the world, walking back from a mall to my hotel room. My entire day had been pretty uneventful, and by far, the most exciting thing that happened to me was this little story.

While I was walking, I felt a sudden sharp pain in my foot. I looked down to find a stick, wedged between my two feet, with a piece of it lodged into the side of my foot. Perplexed, I stood there, stunned for a bit. Did my left foot just stab my right foot?! I pulled out the stick and started limping as I walked to my hotel room.

All of a sudden, a white van screeched to a halt next to me. It was like a scene from a movie. The van door slid open, the windows were rolled down, and I could hear men screaming and yelling. There had to have been about eight men in the van. Two guys ran out of the van DIRECTLY towards me. "RUN," my brain screamed at me. So I started limp-running as fast as I could, until I noticed that the two men had run past me, and I was making a fool of myself. The van door slid shut, and the remaining men drove off into the night.

This story still makes me laugh. I had absolutely no reason to be scared; I knew I was safe in Doha. The stick was far more of a threat, as I ended up with an infection and a remaining sliver that I had to have removed a few weeks later.

# Chapter 13

## How to Meet People

*"If you are traveling alone, cooking in the hostel's kitchen can help you to come in touch with other travelers easily. Inviting others to eat together or catch the sunset together is also a good idea. Ask locals where other locals are going to eat. By this, you will find some nice spots with good food and no tourists."*

- Manuel, Germany

I was in Lagos, Portugal, at a cute little hostel. I had spent the day alone and found myself feeling lonelier than usual. I'd grabbed my laptop and a cheap dinner and decided to try to get some work done on the patio. When I got up there, I noticed a couple of giggling Germans with a bottle of wine. Side note, I love traveling Germans. They are my favorite people to meet in the world. After explaining this to the two Germans, they offered to share their wine and invited me to see the sunset with them. The sunset was happening quickly, and we had to hurry.

Soon, I found myself running as fast as I could with an open bottle of wine. It was such a funny run. All three of us were panting, drinking, laughing, and trying to figure out the quickest route to see the sunset. As we approached the place, I noticed what seemed like a better option and convinced them to try it only to run into a fence. Thanks to me, we missed the sunset, but we did find some pretty cliffs.

## Couchsurfing

Even though I don't use Couchsurfing as a place to sleep anymore, I love to use it to meet new people. There are a couple of ways you can do this and one of such ways is finding local profiles and requesting to hang out or be shown around. This is a great way to meet someone from the city. If they are unable to meet up, just ask for recommendations. Many will happily tell you their favorite restaurants, a good area of town to sleep in, or places to hang out.

The other option is to let others in the city know you want to "hang out." When you turn this function on, you will become one of the many looking for things to do and people to hang out with. You'll see groups that have already formed, and you can ask to join them or you can create your own adventure and wait to see if anyone wants to join yours.

When I was in Spain, I really wanted to go to La Tomatina. La Tomatina is a tomato-throwing festival in the tiny town of Bunol, Spain. Unfortunately, when I got to Valencia, the event was sold out. I got on Couchsurfing and asked the community if they knew where I could get tickets. A fellow couchsurfer with a TON of positive reviews responded and let me know that if I showed up to the event early, there would be a way to buy last minute tickets. He volunteers there every year so he offered to drive me to the location at 4am. After thoroughly reading his reviews, I could see that he was a really good guy. He showed up at my hostel at 4am, as promised, with two other passengers.

We arrived in Bunol an hour later, and my two companions immediately started drinking to pass the time. They offered me some of their beer, and by the time the event started, hours later, we were pretty tipsy. This turned out to be a huge blessing because the La Tomatina event was completely nuts. People were packed in like sardines on one tiny street, tomatoes were everywhere, locals were spraying water from their balconies, and the crowd was singing, yelling, and laughing as the crazy hour ensued.

Afterward, all participants found ways to wash off. I stood in line for showers, only to discover that it was useless against the tomatoes plastered to my body and hair. I eventually climbed into an ice-cold river to wash it off.

It was an unforgettable experience, and I owe it all to my amazing driver. We met up a couple more times while I was in Valencia. He took me to some incredible places for food and showed me some of the favorite local spots.

Couchsurfing has the ability to create these kinds of meaningful and memorable experiences.

## Tours

City Tours are one of the best ways to meet people. Some of my favorite tours include:

**Free Walking Tours:** These tours are usually led by an ex-pat or student. They work on tips, so they are generally friendly and knowledgeable. If they are good, you will learn a lot about the area and be entertained the entire time. You can ask your guide or the people you are with about great local spots to try out while you are in the city.

**Food Tours:** Whoever came up with these is my hero. I love food, meeting people and walking. This does it all. The tour guide will walk you around to local spots where you'll be able to try all kinds of foods and drinks with other tourists. You will often sit down briefly, so it gives you plenty of opportunities to chat with the people around you.

**Pub Crawls:** If you love to drink and meet people, this is a great way to socialize and get to know the nightlife with others. It is easy to get incredibly drunk on these tours, so I'd advise limiting your alcohol initially. You don't want to be that guy or girl who is throwing up halfway through the tour, or do you?

**Ghost Tours:** If you love the thrill of possibly encountering ghosts, these tours can be really fun. They will lead you into old buildings, underground tunnels, graveyards and more.

**Official Tours:** If you go on Trip Advisor, you'll find a ton of tours for most countries. This is a great spot to get information because other travelers rate each tour, so you know what you are getting into.

## Ask to Join Others or for Others to Join You

This used to be hard for me, but as I've gotten older and less worried about what others think, I've come to realize that others are just as nervous and unsure as I am over meeting new people. They want to be liked and to have fun, and most people want a little encouragement. For this reason, I often ask people if they want to join me in whatever I'm doing. "You're welcome to come along." I've even eavesdropped and invited myself to join others.

Just remember that someone always has to be the brave one, "Want to come along?" or "Do you mind if I join you?" It may as well be you. Usually, people will let you know if it isn't possible or be evasive if they don't want you to come. If this happens, just move on and don't take it personally.

It's even possible to find others online that will travel with you for a bit. Try going to either of these websites to plan a trip with someone. Joinmytrip.com or www.workaway.info/en/community/travelbuddy

## What to Ask to Start a Conversation

Be genuine about these questions and listen to the answers. Don't just do it for the sake of trying to meet people, but do it to learn more about them and their travels. Try to listen fully, without trying to impress someone with your own travel experiences. Here are some conversation starters:

- "Excuse me, I'm trying to learn more about___(name of the place you are in.)"

- "Have you guys been able to see much while you've been here?"

- "Where have you gone on your trip? Do you recommend that I see any of those places?"

- "How did you get there?"

- "What will you do for the rest of the day?" "Do you mind if I join you for dinner?"

- "Do you know what kind of nightlife they have here?"

- "Where are you from?"

- "How long have you been traveling?"

- "Do you want to play a drinking game?" (Super common in hostels.)

- "How long have you been traveling."

## Speak Slowly!

Although you will find that everyone tries to communicate using English, you will also notice different levels of proficiency. In most cases, if the person comes from a country that is not a native English-speaking country, you'll need to slow down and articulate more. You can meet some incredible people, but it can be really deterring to people if you are talking away without being aware of how difficult it is to listen to someone speak in a different language. Without meaning to, you can come across rude and self-centered.

From the opposite point of view, I was once in Spain at a hostel and I met a girl from Italy. She couldn't speak English, so she spoke to me in Spanish. I spoke back using what little I knew, and we quickly became friends. My Spanish is extremely limited, so we were not able to have in-depth conversations, but we had so much fun together! She even invited me to visit her in Italy and stay with her family a week later. This would never have happened if she hadn't been patient with me, spoke slowly to me, and overlooked the many times I was simply not able to understand.

## How to Meet Locals

*"Hanging out with someone local will show you much more about a place, and it will be more fun than if you were to go with a guide or hanging out at tourist places."*

- Tal, Israel

Here are some tips on meeting locals:

- Ask hostel workers where to meet them.

- Ask other travelers if they've been able to meet them and how.

- Use Couchsurfing to find local people's profiles and send them messages.

- Look for events going on in the city that are not catered to tourists (festivals, concerts, and such).

- Look to see if there are classes on things you are interested in (yoga, painting, fitness, etc.) Just be ready to use Google translate to let the person know you don't speak their language but will try your best to follow along.

- Sit down at a bar and ask, "How do you say this in __(language.)" (whole phrase in their language.) See if the people will help you learn more.

- Do a homestay. Ask hostels if they know of families taking in travelers for a certain time. You can also use a website to place you. www.homestays.com You'll have to pay for these, but they can be pretty reasonable.

- Use eatwith.com to eat dinner with other travelers and locals. You will pay for these, but it can be a fun way to experience great food.

- Look for language exchange opportunities. I met a ton of people this way while living in Japan. Even if you are only in a city for a short time, this can be a fun way to learn a few new words and meet a local. www.mylanguageexchange.com

- Search for a friend of a friend. Go on social media and see if anyone knows anyone in the place you are visiting that would be willing to show you around a bit.

- Search the internet for ex-pat meetup groups. See if they would be willing to let you come along. The ex-pats will know quite a bit about the city and can often introduce you to the local culture.

- Make conversation on long bus rides or train rides.

- Offer to share your snacks and food.

- Dating apps. I have no desire to use Tinder to meet people, but I have a friend that swears by it. He has some great stories from meeting local women.

- Look for opportunities to participate in the culture. Try things like going to a bath house, getting a haircut or a shave, participate in traditional ceremonies, such as a tea ceremony.

While I was living in China, I decided to get an ombre done on my long dark hair. One of my co-workers said that she knew a guy who could do it, so I trusted that I was in good hands. BIG MISTAKE. A man of about 60 took the bottom half of my hair and bleached it for about 20 minutes, washed it out, and called it good. I looked in the mirror and saw that the majority of my long brown hair was now a bright, ungodly orange color. It took everything I had not to laugh as I paid for the service and walked home. I couldn't wait to see my friend's reaction. All she could do was stare at me and say, "You know I can sugar coat anything, but I have no words for how bad your hair looks." I walked around like that for a few weeks.

Eventually, another co-worker that lived in a nearby city, told me she was dating a hairstylist and he could fix it. The experience in this salon was night and day. The salon had several young, good looking Chinese men ready to help me with my hair. At one point, I had three sets of hands on my hair. It was luxurious, to say the least. True to their word, I looked a lot better when I left.

The guys asked if we wanted to hang out with them that night - they wanted to take us out to a restaurant and then to karaoke. They couldn't speak a word of English, and we could hardly speak any Mandarin. We could only rely on our co-worker. Of course, we went anyway, and it turned out to be a lot of fun. We laughed, sang, ate, drank, and bonded with each other despite the language differences.

# Chapter 14

## Respecting the Culture

*"Always, always, always try to speak a couple of words in the local dialect. Use any words you know! Start with Bonjour, Hola, Hallo, whatever, and you will get respect because you didn't start with, "Do you speak English." If they notice, they might speak English to you, but NEVER expect it! You're in their country; they wouldn't expect you to speak their language when they come to the USA."*

-Sonya, France

While living in Japan, anytime I went out to eat with a bunch of people, I did something I always do when I am at home. I tried to sit in the most inconvenient place at the table to let others get a better seat. In my mind, the person stuck in the middle has the worst seat, and those at the end have the better seat.

It wasn't until several months of living there that I learned I was sitting in the "seat of honor." It is the seat designated for guests, the oldest people in the group, or the ones with the highest career ranking. It was explained to me that they get to sit there because they will not need to get up to serve anyone. I was waltzing right over to it and sitting down every time like, "I'm the guest of honor, people, serve me now!"

While traveling, you will see people living in ways that will be beyond anything you've imagined. Even if you have seen it on TV, there is nothing to prepare you for how it will feel to stand in front of it and experience it first-hand. In some ways, you'll be surprised to see how easily you feel connected to the people in front of you. You will laugh, even when you can't speak each other's language. You will eat delicious food together and feel grateful for it. You will find that basic needs connect you to the culture around you and make you feel a part of it somehow, if only for a moment.

Other times you will feel completely different. You will stare in wonder at things you may not have considered like how women carry their children, how cooking is done, where trash is supposed to go, how people speak to each other (softly, loudly, bluntly), how families sleep at night, how food is collected, what homes look like and so on.

## Manners

"You need to make as much noise as possible!" they told me as I tried to slurp my ramen. "It shows the cook that you appreciate the food." In Japan, it is polite to make a loud, slurping noise when you suck noodles into your mouth. It is NOT an easy sound to imitate without spitting broth all over the place. I was always trying to decide which was ruder, not making enough noise or getting my eating companion drenched.

Each country will have its own set of manners, and it can be difficult to navigate. It is almost impossible not to make some kind of mistake and hope that the person you are speaking to understands that you simply don't know better. Most will understand and explain patiently or giggle, but some will be insulted and expect you to know their rules and customs.

Here is a list of basic manners to keep in mind:

1. Keep your voice down. Try to keep your conversation between you and your group. No one else should be able to hear what you are saying.

2. Be kind. We should do this anyway.

3. Apologize and say thank you, in the local dialect if possible, many times.

4. Ask before taking a picture of a local

## Food

Rule of thumb: if a local puts something in front of you and says it is a delicacy, you do not want to know what it is until after you've eaten it - trust me on this. But unless you want to insult someone thoroughly, you should eat it regardless. There are some things that I have had no intention of ever trying - until I was in front of a table full of local people smiling at me, excited to see if I would like what they made for me. Then I just held my breath and swallowed and said, "mmmm, not bad."

I recommend trying all the foods you can. Local specialties, desserts, street food, even candy bars - try everything. To me, trying new foods is one of the best parts of traveling. I like to research "Top ten things to eat in_" and see what comes up. It's a fun game to try all of the suggested foods.

If you have an allergy, or are vegan or vegetarian, you will need to research before leaving your country. You'll be relieved to know that many places around the world accommodate these things, but it's best to know which ones they are before booking your tickets. I've met many vegans who had to eat meat once or twice because they couldn't find any foods without it. To them, it was worth getting to see the place they were in, but to you, it may not be.

This is a story from a woman named Maureen. She is from the USA but currently resides Israel. She has traveled to many places. Here is her "local delicacy" story.

I lived in Botswana for two years and ate things I had never planned on eating in my life! My first time attending a local village funeral was the first (but not last) time eating ladybugs. I know, horrible right? It was customary to visit the family's house after the ceremony to show respect, which meant sitting and eating a meal with everyone. I was presented with a plate full of Seswaa-meat stew served over Papa. Papa is a maize porridge that is cooked outside in a large black kettle. Well, as I look down at my plate, I see many little ladybugs cooked inside the papa-the downside of cooking in an open kettle in Africa. I was horrified! How could I eat an adorable little ladybug?! But I had to because it would be disrespectful not to. So, I mustered up the courage to eat it-ladybugs and all. A moment I will likely never forget.

## Unsmiling Faces
"They are so rude here!"

Try not to take unsmiling faces, harsh tones, or irritation personally. If you come from a culture that greets each other and exchanges pleasantries with strangers, adapting to being in a culture that doesn't have these customs can be difficult at first. In some countries, someone smiling and being friendly will come across stupid, fake, or suspicious. Observe the ways that locals speak to each other and expect to get the same kind of treatment.

## Bartering

I am an accidental barterer.

Other people bartering: *"That's too much. How about I give you ___ for it. No? Okay,_and that's the highest I'll go."* Hands over money and walks away with purchased satisfied.

Me: *"That's too expensive."* And then I walk away.

Seriously. I just walk right out of the store. It completely baffles shop clerks because they are just doing their jobs. The only advantage of doing this is that sometimes, the store clerks will realize they are about to lose me and call out a lower price. I've accidentally bartered many times this way. It's not nearly as effective as those who call out a lower price and compromise. I'd suggest having two prices in mind: The most you are willing to pay and a lower price to present after a store clerk offers a higher price. You'll find that you either love it or hate bartering, but it is prevalent worldwide, so it's best to be mentally prepared.

## Shopping

The way people shop and sell things is different from country to country, and it can be fun to experience another way of buying things.

In some countries, it's common for store clerks to rush over to help you. They will stand there, practically breathing down your neck, trying to convince you to purchase whatever you are looking at. Maybe it was a turtle that you thought was cute, but you'd never want to own. That turtle will follow you around for the rest of your time in the store. "I'll give you a good price! Only 5! Okay, fine, only 2!"

In some countries, NO ONE will help you. When you finally decide you want to buy it, the customer service person will barely glance up from their phone to ring you up.

In other countries, when you purchase things, you will be expected to bag your own stuff.

In contrast, you will be expected to bring your own bags somewhere else.

You will find salespeople all over the streets trying to sell you their stuff in many places. They compete with each other, so they will get in your face trying to get your attention before any of their competitors try first. It can be overwhelming at first, but you will soon get used to it. This is why I'm so practiced at keeping my head low and saying, "No." I ignore things like, "You didn't even look!"

Yet, in other places, salespeople will follow you for a while, trying to make conversation and hoping you will eventually cave. I once had a woman follow me for over an hour in a tiny village outside Sapa, Vietnam. She had her baby strapped to her back, and she patiently followed and talked to me about where I was and the history and details of her people. I was irritated at first but realized that she had nothing better to do and was simply doing her job. After an hour, I was carrying half her stuff for her and talking back. I only ended up buying a small bag from her because I knew I was being manipulated, but I did appreciate her tenacity.

The next day, I found myself laughing when I saw her and a few other townspeople following another group of tourists. The tourists made eye contact with me like, "Help!" and the woman looked at me like, "I got another one!" I learned later that they made a lot of money that way.

# Bathrooms

Here are a few wise words from my father; heed his advice: "RESTROOM TRIPS, DON'T DRINK TOO MUCH COFFEE BEFORE GOING OUT TO SIGHTSEE." - ELDON.

When it comes to bathrooms in foreign countries, you really never know what you are going to get. In order to be prepared, carry change in case it costs money, hand sanitizer, and tissues. Many places don't offer toilet paper, and some don't even have running water to wash your hands. Another thing to keep in mind is that many countries require people to throw used toilet paper in trash cans rather than in toilets. Typically, this is due to old plumbing. I ALWAYS ask when I'm somewhere new.

There are all sorts of toilets in the world, but it really comes down to two different kinds, the kind you sit on and the kinds you squat over. In some places, you'll wish they had something to sit on. In others, it will be so dirty that you'll wish you had somewhere to squat. I'll spare you the details of the disgusting toilet situations I've seen.

Here are two hilarious stories about bathroom adventures in China.

### Story 1

When my friend and I first moved to China, she had never used a squatty toilet before. She decided to brave it and she went in. She came out and said it went fine, but she was a little confused. "What is the basket that is in the middle of it?" I had no idea what she was talking about, so I glanced in her stall and just died laughing. It was the trash basket. Somehow, it had gotten in the squatty basin. Since she had no idea what a squatty was supposed to look like, she just did her business ON TOP OF the trash can!!

### Story 2

Once my mom was visiting me in China, so we decided to go to a mall together. We needed to use the restroom, and all they had were squatting toilets. At this point, I'd traveled to several countries that had these, and I was pretty comfortable using them, but I knew that they could be intimidating to people at first. I assured my mom that she would be fine, so she went in. Less than 2 minutes later, she came flying out with a mortified look on her face and yelled, "Go! Go! Go! Go!" We quickly moved along, and then she explained what happened. Apparently, she had "aimed" incorrectly and missed the toilet entirely. The contents had rolled out of the toilet stall and onto the floor. There were two women in there with her, so she panicked and ran out of the bathroom without even washing her hands! We were laughing so hard, and it is something that she will likely never live down.

Things NOT to do while in a different country:

- DON'T compare cultures: "In my country we____." It is often a way to relate and connect to the person, but instead, it sounds like the person isn't appreciating what is going on in front of them or wants to draw the conversation to themselves. Wait until you are asked before sharing.

- DON'T belittle or make fun of the culture you are in - this is one of my biggest pet peeves - These kinds of people rarely ever fully comprehend the culture they are judging, and they sound like idiots to anyone listening with a fraction of cultural awareness.

- DON'T treat the country or people like you are above them, their laws, or their customs. This is probably one of the most common things I've seen and is typically done by younger travelers. They are loud, often drunk, and sometimes drastically unaware of how offensive and inconsiderate they are being. If they are aware of it, they don't care and think it's funny. It's not just US citizens who do this, but we are known for it all over the world.

- DO appreciate the culture you are in, pay attention to the things you like, and avoid picking apart the things you don't like.

- DO remember that one culture is not better than the other. It's different.

- DO try to keep your personal, religious, or political beliefs to yourself unless you are specifically asked.

- DON'T comment on a country's leaders, political climate, tensions, mistakes, history, or economic status unless you are asked. Many people do this to sound knowledgeable, or to relate, but many other cultures out there do not openly discuss these things - especially not with strangers. Try to understand that, at the very least, you could insult them or make them uncomfortable. You may even put them in danger by openly discussing your criticism for their leadership.

- DO be patient with those who will openly discuss the country you are from and tell you what they like and don't like. If you believe that your country is the best, the world will openly let you know why they disagree. Try to listen, learn, grow, or at the very least, don't be defensive.

- DON'T assume that because a country has many "poor people," they are not happy or living full lives. Telling them that you feel sorry for them is unacceptable, and it doesn't always make sense. People who live simple lives with little money are just as capable of living wonderful, happy lives full of love and purpose.

# Chapter 15
## Getting the Most Out of Your Trip

## Attitude

Recently, my friend Krystal shared with me that she got stuck in a stairwell in Las Vegas. She went through a door, hoping it would lead her out, and then it locked behind her. The pattern kept happening and she eventually found herself in an underground tunnel between two major hotels. She said it smelled like urine and was filled with cockroaches. She was freaking out, but luckily her phone was working. She was able to call her husband, who had no idea where she'd gone. He tried to get the hotel to help, but he kept getting passed over to other people. It took about 30 minutes for him to get help.

As she told me her story, I realized that she was completely distressed by the occasion. I was nodding and making sympathizing noises until she got to the part where her husband said, "My wife is stuck in a stairwell!" and for whatever reason, this struck me funny, and I laughed.

My poor friend was looking for sympathy, but all I could think about was how bizarre the situation was, and it just made me laugh. Her husband had to repeat the phrase several times, and it each time she repeated it, it became even funnier. When they finally found her, they tried to play a joke on her by pretending not to be able to open the last door. At that point, she had reached her limit, and it did not go over well.

Listening to her tell the story was like watching a comedy sketch. I was cracking up, and I'm lucky she has a good sense of humor because she didn't find it too amusing at the time when she was telling me the story. I've had her tell the story a few times, and she can finally laugh when she tells it now.

Attitude can make or break any situation. Just like most typical days, traveling days are filled with ups and downs. Humor can be found in almost any situation - it's just a matter of time and perspective. Time is needed to process negative emotions, and perspective is required to perceive a negative experience as part of an adventurous journey rather than an incident that ruined the day.

Here are some tips for keeping a good attitude while traveling:

- **Find the story:** Look for ways to make a good story out of any frustration. "You should have seen your face when the guy told us we were on the wrong train."

- **Look for reasons to be grateful:** Be prepared to make some kind of mistake. Remember that problems have a way of working themselves out. "It will turn out fine. I can't believe how lucky I am to be walking on this street."

- **Avoid Complaining:** Especially out loud. It brings you and your entire group down. "It's hot." "Why is this line so long??" "I told you we should have eaten first." "Why do they need 100 selfies?" Try to find the good things instead.

- **Make others a part of your story:** A friend and I always had nicknames for the people we met. Mostly positive, but we did have a few nicknames that still make us laugh when we look back. We once met a drunk guy who would not stop blathering on about wines. My friend is one of the most polite people you will ever meet, so she listened to him throughout his entire speech. We ended up calling him "Wine Tour" for the rest of the trip. We hung out with him once again later, and he was nice when he was sober, but when he got drunk again, my friend casually leaned over and mentioned, "Wine Tour's back."

- **BREATH!** Don't forget to stop and take deep breaths - when you see something beautiful, when a moment captures your heart, when you are overwhelmed with emotions, when you are frustrated with someone or yourself, or when you are so overjoyed by what you see that you feel your heart might burst - breathe! Take 1-3 deep breaths and let that moment be yours.

## Traveling with Others

When I first started traveling, I traveled with my best friend - someone who easily laughs, is excited about everything, and loves adventure as much as I do. She set the bar high for a travel partner. She was always conscientious of her surroundings, respectful of her environment, and had a great attitude. It was so easy with her that I find myself hesitating to travel with other people. She is the reason I know that traveling with someone else can be an amazing experience.

I won't spend too much time convincing you that traveling with others can be great because if you are like most people, you will prefer to start traveling this way. If you decide to travel with others, here are some tips:

1. Split everything from the beginning and pay each other back as you go. It makes it so much easier than trying to tally everything up at the end. Someone always ends up paying more because it's difficult to remember what you've spent along the way. Use Venmo or similar cash apps to split

hotels, restaurant tabs, and tours. Trust me - everyone will be a lot happier.

2. Make sure everyone involved has the financial means to pay for everything planned on the trip. This can eliminate unpleasant encounters between travel partners.

3. Be communicative. Remember the saying, "Communication is key?" It most certainly is!

4. Be okay with doing something on your own. There will be times when one person will want to do something different. Separate and then come back together and share what happened when you were alone.

5. Choose travel buddies that you enjoy hanging out with at home. You are about to experience some amazing things together, but you will also have moments of confusion, stress, irritability, and exhaustion. You want that person to be someone who understands that you will not always be in the best mood and vise versa.

## Record, Record, Record

My best friend and I always write down our funniest stories, quotes, and situations. We try to record them the same day they happened so we don't forget. Neither of us uses journals, so our stories stay pretty small and summarized to a few sentences. I've used these stories to make a couple of picture books of our trips, and I included the quotes and stories at the end. The pictures are always nice to look at, but those quotes remind us of the day-to-day part of our trip that could easily be forgotten.

Don't assume you'll remember everything. So many times, I've forgotten a story until I look back at the album.

What kinds of things to keep track of:

- **Funny interactions:** "He didn't ask if you wanted to see an iguana; he asked if you wanted marijuana!"

- **The names of foods you tried:** Borscht in Poland, Ceviche in Peru, Okonomiyaki in Japan

- **The people you met and their contact info:** This is helpful in case you decide to meet up again later in life. Unlikely, but it could happen. Social Media keeps you connected the best these days.

- **Other travelers' suggestions:** "Tom from NZ says to go to ___ for dinner." "Krystal says that Szimpla Kert was her favorite ruin bar in Budapest."

- **What you are missing about home:** Remind yourself of the small things to be grateful for when you return. "I miss my giant comfy bed!"

- **Things you are grateful for:** "I'm grateful for beer and pretty views."

- **Places you visited, things you experienced, and views you saw:** "Today we arrived in Tamarindo. We walked along the beach and spontaneously took a river tour with a local on his boat. We were able to see crocodiles, wild birds, and stunning plant life as we sipped beer and enjoyed the ride. At one point, my brother tripped and nearly fell off the boat."

## Prepare for Reverse-Culture Shock

I'm convinced that everyone goes through a minor reverse-culture shock upon returning home from a good trip. The longer you are away, the harder it is to return - especially when you realize that you can't take the life you just experienced home with you. When you return, you'll find everything is the same as when you left it. People at home will not be able to fully understand what you just experienced, and it can be a lonely time for a traveler.

One of the hardest things to be prepared for is the lack of interest that others have in your trip. Be prepared to summarize your entire life-altering experience with one or two adjectives. Those who are perceptive and want to know more will ask, but most will not want to hear more than, "It was great." Try not to be too hard on those you love for this. Instead, look for ways to meet travelers that reside in your area. You can seek out friends, friends of friends, or meet travelers on apps such as *couchsurfing.com* and *Meetup.com*.

For those who spent months or even years living or traveling overseas, coming home isn't just hard - it's a grieving process. It's like a death; the life you just lived can't come home with you. After returning, most people have no idea that this feeling of loss occurs and wanders around for months in a daze, wondering what on earth is wrong with themselves. The people in their lives will be confused because they will expect someone who just got back from traveling to be full of life, stories, and wisdom. Instead, a traveler comes home and feels torn between worlds and no longer has a sense of belonging anywhere.

Someone who is mentally prepared to grieve the life they lived will do much better than someone who returns and can't explain to others or themselves what is wrong. If you do decide to go anywhere, embrace those difficult emotions that come when you return. They are normal.

*"How lucky I am to have something that makes saying goodbye so hard".*

- Winnie the Pooh

The last story I'll share in this book is about a hilarious and miserable experience riding a slow-overnight train. As with all of the stories in this book, I hope it will inspire you to travel, to find humor in all your adventures, and to go out and create your own crazy, amazing, and memorable stories.

While living in a foreign country, that I'm purposely not naming because most experiences in this country are NOT like this, three of us friends decided to take a long-distance train to get to another city. We booked the train hoping for sleeper cars, but we waited too long, and the only options available were the cheapest seats. We were okay; we assumed that it would be similar to most long-distance trains.

We were wrong.

Each aisle had seats that faced each other. Three seats on one side and two seats on the other. The table was tiny, and the seats were extremely close together, so it was impossible not to touch the other person's legs that were sitting across from you. If people can't afford the seats they will find places to sit and stand in the aisles.

We were crammed into tiny spaces on a train filled with mostly men, who were either sprawled out sleeping in any position you can think of - or wide awake and staring directly at us. Thirteen hours is a LONG time to sit on a train with men watching your every move. They leaned over seats, turned around to see our pictures, watched us talk, sleep, wake up, get up, and eat with steady stares and unabashed curiosity.

All three of us have funny stories. Me with the cockroaches climbing near my head and the lady next to me trying to sing me to sleep. My other friend being shuffled around all night by people who kept waking her up to ask her to move. And my third friend, who kept getting kicked in the butt by the guy across from her, to which she finally tapped him and motioned for his feet to stop kicking her in the butt. At one point, I woke up and realized I'd just kicked a man in the head. He'd laid himself under our impossibly small table on the floor to sleep.

The experience was nuts. Men took off their shoes and put their feet everywhere. The man across from me even put his feet on my legs! It was nothing personal or creepy. This is just how they sleep.

If they weren't sleeping, they didn't have a lot of regard for those who were trying to sleep. They spoke loudly, blew snot into trash cans, made loud noises trying to clean the gunk out of their throats, and spit into trash cans. Foreigners are rare in those parts, so they would, at times, surround us in a non-threatening way to discuss us like animals in a zoo.

We rode for 26 hours in total, and while we all three still laugh about the insanity of it, we vowed to never put ourselves through that again. The friends I had on this trip are both fantastic travelers. This experience would not have been the same without them. I am so grateful to have shared this experience with two people I trusted to have a good sense of humor - we seriously needed it.

## It's your turn! Go out and create your own stories and advice!!

# Extras

## Tips from Other Travelers

I've sprinkled some of these tips throughout the book, but I only had room for so many. I've been so lucky to have met such wonderful travelers along the way, and many of them took time to write down stories and advice for this book. Here is every single traveler that took time to respond and their words.

## Jenny from Canada

"Walk around anywhere that you are going with a purpose. Look like you know where you are going and that you have to be somewhere, even if you are totally lost. I feel that you are less likely to be taken advantage of. Resting bitch face may help as well! Lol."

## Kenisa from the USA

"Don't plan more than 50% of your time. Leave time for navigational errors, random explorations on locals/hosts' recommendations, and sometimes time to just relax or take a nap. Our trips are so much better when we have lots of flexibility in our schedule. We try to plan one thing per day, and everything else is spontaneous. We make lists of maybes/things we are interested in but will only do them if time allows."

"Always bring snacks with you, so you're not stuck hungry, trying to find someplace to eat in an unfamiliar place. I always think there will be more quick-stop food places on our routes than there actually are."

"Always have just enough cash, but not too much because of those sneaky pick-pocketers you always read about) It's a delicate balance. Little bars in little towns out in the middle of nowhere don't always have credit card machines and trying to find some way to pull cash when literally the rest of the town is asleep is not fun.

Especially when you are hungry, see the above tip. Not speaking from experience or anything."

## Sarah from Canada

"Just do it!" (travel)

"Always pack less than what you think you need. You don't need that cute outfit you might wear that one night. Once you're there, it won't matter!"

## Tomoko from Japan

"Appreciate being able to travel."

"Talk to locals as much as you can, join the local events, and respect their culture."

"Make empty space for souvenirs you might receive."

## Jessica Donley from New Orleans, USA

"When we step out, with trusting hearts, into the unknown, we become magnets for blessings!"

## Anna from New Zealand

"You don't have to be rich to travel; some of the best experiences can be found with people you meet in a hostel dorm or campground."

"Don't be afraid to go somewhere you don't know the language. You can start with a thumbs up, pointing, and a smile."

## Jon from Switzerland who grew up all over the world

"Just go!"

"Look for local train deals. Sometimes they are much cheaper than express deals. Like from the London airport or the Glacier Express to Switzerland. You can do the exact same thing on local trains for way less money."

## Manuel from Germany

"If you are traveling on a low budget, try to cook for yourself. But in most Asian countries, it's cheaper to eat out."

"If you are traveling alone, cooking in the hostel's kitchen can help you come in touch with other travelers easily."

"Inviting others to eat together or catch the sunset together is also a good idea."

"Ask locals where other locals are going to eat. By this, you will find some nice spots with good food and no tourists."

"If you want to catch the sunset, take a bottle (or two) of wine with you. But better start 15 minutes earlier than too late." (side note, he and his friend Julie are the ones I lead the wrong way while in Lagos.)

"Look for hostels you want to go to next. Sometimes it's hard to get a spot in a hostel, so you should try to book it before. But if this is not the case, you can travel there and look for a nice hostel on location."

"Try to get in touch with other travelers; they often have good advice for hostels, spots you should see, hidden places, and good restaurants."

## Elinor - born in the UK but grew up in Denmark

"You don't need as many things as you think you do. I've lived for literally years with only one small backpack, and it felt like the ultimate freedom. Sure, you get bored wearing the same clothes a lot, but you can always swap it out at a charity shop, etc., and it's so worth it when you don't have to lug a heavy suitcase from point A-B every time you go somewhere new. It also makes flights super cheap if you can get away with just hand luggage in Europe."

"The experience of meeting new people and creating new connections is something you learn along the way - don't be discouraged if your first solo travel experience felt hard because it definitely gets easier over time."

"Don't plan your trip from start to finish; leave space for outside influences, so you can go with the flow."

"A great place to start if you are on a budget is a workaway/helpx/WOOFing experience. You save money because you are working for food and lodging, you get to spend more time in one place (usually not a tourist destination), and it can be a really good place to meet new people-either a local family, or like-minded travelers that are also there."

## Lisa from the USA
"Always bring toilet paper. If you're in a rush, you may zip past the place to buy toilet paper without realizing it." (many countries charge for using restrooms or toilet paper. Always have some tissues on you!)

## Laura from Germany
"No expectations. It's never like what you expect it will be."

## Carmen from the USA but grew up in multiple countries
Carmen has a blog called "5 Ways NOT to be a Tourist." At whereindaworld.com, it highlights some of the ways someone can travel, like visiting friends, working overseas, volunteering, etc. I highly recommend checking her blog out. She has traveled extensively and has amazing advice and stories.

## Faira from Kuwait
"Try searching for flights in Incognito mode - you might be able to find cheaper flights. Also, look up the best times to buy tickets. I've heard it's 1 am."

## Chelsea from the USA
"Leave the laptop and take the Pepto. Also, bring garbage bags to put your suitcase in, in case there are bedbugs."

## Sonya from France and lives in the USA

"Keep business cards from restaurants." (for scrapbooks, recommendations, or to revisit)

"Restaurants are fun and good, but grocery stores will be MUCH cheaper, and I've had so many more fun layovers (flight attendant) having a picnic in the Luxembourg Gardens or Champ de Mars (next to the Eiffel Tower) than I have at overpriced and overrated restaurants! And since you can drink in a park there, don't forget the Madiran! (Underrated red wine from SW of France!) No need to spend to have fun! Picnicking will allow you to sit next to strangers and maybe make friends! Although if you want to meet locals, Eiffel Tower's probably not your best bet, haha!"

"I love to just walk around a foreign city and get lost, and venture into that shop that looks like a mom and pop's at the "Galries Lafayettes" because you read about it in a travel magazine. Find things out for yourself! When you go to mom and pop shops, ask THEM where to go for dinner or what to do, not your travel guide written by an American who was there for a week."

"Put your phone down. Don't ask Siri. ASK locals!"

"Always, always, always try to speak a couple of words in the local dialect. Use any words you know! Start with Bonjour, Hola, Hallo, whatever, and you will get respect because you didn't start with, "Do you speak English?" If they notice, they might speak English to you, but NEVER expect it! You're in their country; they wouldn't expect you to speak their language when they come to the USA."

## Ben from the USA
"It's not wrong to bring skis all year, everywhere, just in case."

## Linchie from India who lives in the UK
"I'm surprised by how often people forget the essential medicines and international adapters for charging."

"It doesn't hurt to carry extra underwear, t-shirts, or jeans in your handbag. Saved us once in Bali when our airlines didn't deliver our luggage for two days."

## Estee from the USA

"Always do some research before traveling, and definitely respect the cultural differences."

"Limit the amount of crap you bring with you; it will help tremendously!"

"If something is offered to you, out of kindness by a local, always accept it. Whether it's food, a drink, a ceremony invite, or a recommended spot to visit, if they're kind enough to offer, always accept."

As they were dropping me off, the woman got motherly and told me, "NEVER EVER get in a car with strangers in Brazil. Please be more careful! It's okay because you're with me, but please be safe." Then she gave me a huge hug and left me at my hotel.

## Maya from South Africa

"Just start traveling and don't be scared. I've been to many places that people would consider dangerous, and I have felt very safe."

## Amy from the USA

"Know what bed bugs look like because any hotel or hostel—whether it's more upscale or rundown—can have bed bugs if the previous traveler before you brought them there. If you're unsure about whether a hotel will be good to stay at or not, you can always ask to see your room before you pay for it. Don't put your luggage on the bed when first entering your room. Inspect the inside of the pillows and lift up the fitted sheet to see the sides of the mattress to check for bed bugs and the telltale spots from their activity. Also, listen to your intuition. I usually research where to stay beforehand but ended up needing to find a hotel room quickly and unexpectedly when a volcano eruption resulted in my evening flight out of Indonesia getting canceled. It was already 11 pm in the evening so I didn't have time to do very much research and ended up in a hotel room that was quite run down and (unbeknownst to me at the time) was infested with bed bugs. I had never come across any bed bugs and didn't know what they looked like, but in retrospect, I saw one crawl over the pillow and onto the bedspread within the first few minutes of being in that room. I had an uneasy feeling but told myself that it was only for one night. I unpacked as little as possible and tried to get some sleep. But somehow, my intuition knew something was off because at 3 am, I had a strong feeling that I needed to leave ASAP. Luckily, I listened to the feeling, packed up my stuff (putting everything that I had unpacked into a ziplock bag), called a taxi, and went to another hotel. I asked to see the room at the new hotel before paying for it. As I prepared to take a shower, that was when I found a bed bug crawling on the inside of my thigh. I shrieked and managed to trap it under a glass so I could identify what it was. Needless to say, I learned everything that you could possibly know about bed bugs that night and didn't sleep a wink scrutinizing every single belonging in my luggage in detail to ensure I didn't bring back any."

"I like to bring my own eating utensils (travel chopsticks or UCO utility spork) with me so I can easily have a meal in my hotel room or a picnic somewhere outside. Also, it's great if you're at a restaurant or place where you're not sure if the eating utensils provided are clean. "

"One time, I got food poisoning on a long international flight. I got really dehydrated throughout the flight and asked the flight attendants desperately for some electrolyte solution like Gatorade but unfortunately, they didn't have anything. I realized after the fact that I could have combined salt and sugar together in some juice, coconut water, or water with lemon juice in a pinch. I now always carry little packs of Pedialyte in my mini first aid/medications kit just in case; they are also useful for after motion sickness bouts or hangovers. "

## Zerene from India

"Be considerate of which country you're going to and their clothing."

"Never let anyone pick up your luggage, even at the airport, from the luggage belt. Once, this guy helped me pick up my bag from the luggage belt. I thought he was so kind and then he asked for money for helping me. So, no strangers pick up my bag no matter what."

## Steve from the USA
"Travel with a Lanyard" (to hold keys)

"Take a left on a street when you should take a right to get where you're going."

"Get on a subway, bus, or trolley. Go 45 minutes in any direction to outside of a normal tourist spot. Get off at a random spot and just wander around."

"Google Maps shows good neighborhoods walking areas in a shade of beige."

"Budget flights can be more expensive than normal flights if you check bags."

"Bathe like locals. In some countries, public bathing is relaxing and more spiritual. Get out of western thoughts about bathing."

"Find something you notice that all people do, but that might be done differently in different cultures, and then seek out that experience when you travel. For example, bathing, getting a shave, drinking tea, or drinking coffee."

"If you are on a budget, take an uber to a close bus line, and you can save a ton of money."

"If you miss something, don't worry. You can always come back."

"If you are traveling for more than 14-30 days, take a vacation from your traveling."

"Walking tours are great!"

## Nick from Australia
"Learn a few basic words in the language of the country you're in as an easy way to be respectful."

"Eat and drink what the locals are eating and drinking!"

## Augusto from Peru

"I don't wear fancy clothing when I travel, and I don't show off."

"Do some research on the country's laws. Some laws are very strict."

## Ebony from the USA

"Before I plan a trip, I think about my expectations for the trip. Do I want to relax? Do I want to explore with the locals? Or do I want to hit all of the tourist attractions? I also make sure to align these expectations with my travel companions. This helps limit disagreements on what activities to do on our trip."

## Justin from EVERYWHERE (USA, Scotland, Italy, Australia)

"Traveling is one of life's greatest experiences. It broadens the mind and builds character. My advice is to listen and learn wherever you go. When I travel, I enjoy seeing how people live, love, work, learn, and compare how they're different. I tend to consider what I can take from these experiences back with me, and it can be life-changing."

"I think it's really important to meet the local people. My word of advice is to try to make a new friend in every place that you visit."

## Julie from Germany

"Don't always listen to what other people tell you. If I'd listened to what other people had told me, I would have missed out on so many great adventures. There was this one time when I planned on traveling to Morocco with a friend. He had an accident a few days before we left and he couldn't go. I decided to go by myself. Everyone told me horror stories they had heard somewhere, but not one of these people was ever in Morocco. I went and had the best three weeks. I met wonderful people and didn't have a single inappropriate or strange encounter."

"Be respectful! If you need to wear a crop top and hot pants while traveling, don't go to a Muslim country. "

"Be open-minded! Be open when it comes to food, people, and culture!"

"Hostel bars or common areas are the places to be when you want to meet people. Don't be shy, talk to them, and you'll make friends for life. (I've met so many great people while traveling, you are one of them!)

## Paulien from The Netherlands
"My advice is to buy a LifeStraw bottle. IT makes it possible to drink water from tap everywhere. At the same time, you save the world from using a lot of single-use plastic.

## Ryan from the USA
"Travel is so life-giving! You get to explore, see new things, meet new people, experience new things, and one of my favorites, it helps you connect with other people. A connection is based on common experiences. So if I visit a certain state or country and someone is from there or has been there, I share an experience, and it brings a connection. We are made for connection in relationships, and traveling is a great way to connect."

"For so long, I thought traveling was a lot, and it wouldn't be restful because there are so many details. I changed my perspective, and with technology today, it is easy to book a room, flight, or an adventure all online. Once you get into a travel rhythm, it is just like anything in life. It becomes natural. It is easy to hop on a flight, get an uber, get a hotel, or go on an adventure. Hope you don't hold back and just go for it!"

## Tal from Israel
"Don't disregard connections with like-minded people that you meet along the way. No matter how slim the chance that you will

meet again. And don't be afraid to reach out when you're in the neighborhood."

"Hanging out with someone local will show you much more about a place, and it will be more fun than if you were to go with a guide or hanging out at tourist places."

## Charlotte from the UK

"Always carry tiger balm for mosquito bites, mosquito repellent, burns, headache relief, and stuff for a bad chest/nose."

Eldon from the USA

"Restroom trips: Don't drink too much coffee before going out to sightsee."

## Elinor from the UK

"For me, at least, the biggest benefit has been the people I've met through it. And since you've got food and accommodation covered, Workaways allow you to stay somewhere for two weeks, a month (or even six months in my experience), wwhich is enough time to really get to know a place and bond with other people that you're with. Also, for people who are a bit shy and who wouldn't like the "forwardness" of meeting people in a hostel dorm, a workaway experience can provide a really nice environment to meet new people more calmly.

It's a great chance to learn new skills! My partner once stayed with a family that taught him glass-blowing - how cool is that?!

Right now, I am living in a tiny village in the Italian mountains, and the only reason I know this village even exists isthat I came here for a workaway three years ago. There's literally no other reason to go here. It's not even connected with public transport, but it's a beautiful place and there's a great workaway connected community here that's usually got 15-20 people living in the same old house all summer. It's an absolute gem, and I'm sure there are many work/volunteer places that are similar in some way.

I would say that before you go anywhere, make sure you've read what they want in exchange for food and lodging, and make sure it feels fair to you. The standard is 5/hours for 5 days (so 25/hours total), and in my opinion, they should provide both lodging and food (or money to buy food, I've had a place like that as well.)

But some places are looking for cheap labor, and you can usually tell by their profile and their reviews. If worst comes to worst, you can always leave.

There are a lot of "Voluntourism" scams. It's worth being mindful that you are not taking away work from the local community if you are volunteering in a third world country. Personally, I would likely not do a workaway in a third world country unless I know it's 100 percent legit, but that is a subjective opinion.

Another thing I've done a lot in the past year is house-sitting: looking after people's pets in exchange for staying rent-free in their home when they are away. It's great for people who want a change of scenery for a few weeks. It's obviously a lot less social, so it's more suited for people traveling as a coupleor people working remotely. It's a great money saver, for example, you could stay in the middle of London for two weeks without paying anything, and all you have to do is look after someone's cat!"

# Basic Packing List

| Clothing | Toiletries | Electronic | Documents | Extras |
|----------|-----------|-----------|-----------|--------|
| ☐ Shirts | ☐ Toothbrush, Paste, Dental Floss | ☐ Travel Adapter and Converter | ☐ Passport Tickets for Airline, Boat, Train, or Buses | ☐ Medication, Pain Reliever |
| ☐ Tank Tops | | | | ☐ Insect Repellent |
| ☐ Pants | ☐ Deodorant | ☐ Camera, Memory Card, Charger | ☐ Copies of Passports | ☐ Birth Control |
| ☐ Skirts | ☐ Tweezers | | | |
| ☐ Dresses | ☐ Soap, Shampoo, Conditioner | ☐ Laptop, iPad, E-Readers | ☐ Driver's License | ☐ Hand Sanitizer |
| ☐ Shorts | | | | |
| ☐ Sleepwear | ☐ Travel Towel | | ☐ Health Insurance Card | ☐ Day Pack |
| ☐ Underwear | ☐ Nailcare | ☐ Chargers | | ☐ Language Guide |
| ☐ Socks/ Stockings | ☐ Tissues | ☐ Headphones | ☐ Student ID | |
| | | | | ☐ Purse |
| | ☐ Feminine Hygiene | ☐ Hair utensils | ☐ Journal | |
| ☐ Swimsuit | | | ☐ Itinerary | ☐ Money Belt, safety whistle |
| ☐ Sandals | ☐ Makeup | | | |
| ☐ Shoes/ Sneakers | ☐ Shaving Supplies | | ☐ Maps and Directions | ☐ Packing Cubes! |
| ☐ Jacket/ Raincoat/ Coat | ☐ Skin Care | | | ☐ Eye Mask |
| | ☐ Sunscreen | | | ☐ Ear Plugs |
| ☐ Scarves, Hats, Gloves | ☐ Brush, Comb, Hair Products | | | ☐ Sleeping Pills |
| | | | | ☐ Plastic Bags, Ziplock Storage Bags |
| | ☐ Glasses, Contacts, Supplies | | | ☐ Tissues or Wet Wipes |
| | ☐ Lotion | | | ☐ Dry Bag |
| | ☐ Hair Ties and Accessories | | | ☐ Hand lock for Bags or Lockers |

# Traveler's Checklist

## 1. Purchase Tickets

- [ ] Write down date of departure
- [ ] Write down flight number
- [ ] Write down layover location and times
- [ ] Write down final destination
- [ ] Call airline or book seat selection online

## 2. Place of Lodging

- [ ] Write down the name of lodging and the address
  (You will need this to enter the country)
- [ ] Write down the names of other places you will stay

## 3. Transportation

- [ ] Write down how you will get from the airport to your lodging (bus, taxi, shuttle)
- [ ] How much will the transportation cost?
- [ ] Map out the route from the airport and screenshot it to refer to if Wi-Fi isn't available.
- [ ] Research different modes of transportation you will use while you are visiting.
  Which ones will you take?  What is the average cost for each?

## 4. Rental Car

- [ ] How much will it cost?  What extra fees should you expect?
- [ ] What will you need to drive? (I.D., passport info, etc...)
- [ ] How will you get an International Driver's License (In person, online.)
- [ ] How will you document the condition of the vehicle BEFORE you drive it
  (video, pictures are highly recommended.)

## 5. Activity

☐ What will you do when you get there?

☐ Do you need to book tickets or tours ahead of time?

## 6. Money

☐ How much do you plan to spend a day?

☐ What is the converted amount? (ex: what is $100 to yen?)

☐ Call bank and credit card companies to notify them you'll be out of the country

☐ Make sure there will be an ATM in the airport so you can pull out some cash right away. You may need it for transportation.

## 7. Translation and Language

☐ What language do the people of the country you are visiting speak?

☐ How to say.... Hello - Sorry - Thank you - Please - Where - Numbers 1-10

☐ How will I translate? (Language dictionary, Google Translate, translation app)

## 8. Passport

Do you have a passport?

☐ Yes

o Does it expire within 6 months of the departure date?

o Are there some blank pages?

☐ No

o What steps will you take to get it ready in time?

## 9. Visa

☐ How long are you allowed to stay in the country you are visiting? (90, 180 days etc...)

☐ Does the place you are visiting require a special visa process for citizens of your country?

o How will you complete the visa (Online, in person, company)

o What documents do you need to turn in for the visa?

o What documents will you need with you to get through immigration?

o Does the country require an entry fee? Does it have to be in local cash?

## 10. Theft and Scam Prevention

- [ ] Do you have printed copies of your passport? Photo ID? Flight Information?
- [ ] Have you hidden a card in a separate place?
- [ ] What is your anti-theft plan (small purse, wallet in front, money belt)
- [ ] What are the emergency numbers for the country you are visiting? (911)

## 11. Sim Cards and VPNs

- [ ] Do you want to purchase data while overseas?

  If yes, will you buy a SIM card to be delivered to you or wait until you get there?
- [ ] Will you need a VPN?

  o What service will you use?

  o Is it month to month?

  o Can you cancel it when you no longer need it?

## 12. Vaccines and Prescriptions

- [ ] What vaccines do you need to visit the country or region you are visiting?
- [ ] Do you have enough of your prescriptions to last the entire trip?
- [ ] If you have allergies, do you have what you need? (Epi-pen, inhaler, etc)
- [ ] Do you have food allergies? Research places and things you can eat.

## 13. Apps

- [ ] What apps will you download before leaving?

## 14. Plane

- [ ] What will you bring on the plane to make your ride more comfortable?
- [ ] What movies or books will you bring with you?
- [ ] What snacks will you bring?
- [ ] What custom forms are required to be filled out upon arrival?

  Can you get them ahead of time?

## 15. Recording Details

- [ ] How will you record the small details of my trip that you don't want to forget?

  (Journal, app, phone, pictures)

## 16. Clothing and Modesty Standards

☐ What clothing restrictions does the country have that you are visiting?

(shorts, skirts, shoulders showing)

☐ How do other travel bloggers say to dress?

(modest, doesn't matter)

Made in United States
Orlando, FL
27 November 2024

54546891R00100